# SHORTCUT 1

# 408 HEALING QUOTES

by LINKED IN AND TOWN HALL ACHIEVER OF THE YEAR
EY NOMINEE ENTREPRENEUR OF THE YEAR
GRAND HOMAGE US DIVERSITY
WORLD TOP100 DOCTORS

## Dr BAK NGUYEN, DMD

TO ALL THOSE LOOKING TO MOVE ON FROM THE PAST
WITH HOPE FOR A BETTER FUTURE

by Dr BAK NGUYEN

ISBN: 978-1-989536-73-5

Published by: Dr. BAK PUBLISHING COMPANY
**Dr.BAK 0093**

# DISCLAIMER

« The general information, opinions and advice contained in this medium and/or the books, audiobooks, podcasts and publications on Dr. Bak Nguyen's (legal name Dr. Ba Khoa Nguyen) website or social media (hereinafter the "Opinions") present general information on various topics. The Opinions are intended for informational purposes only.

No information contained in the Opinions is a substitute for an expert, consultation, advice, diagnosis or professional treatment. No information contained in the Opinions is a substitute for professional advice and should not be construed as consultation or advice.

Nothing in the Opinions should be construed as professional advice related to the practice of dentistry, medical advice or any other form of advice, including legal or financial advice, professional opinion, care or diagnosis, but strictly as general information. All information from the Opinions is for informational purposes only.

Any user who disagrees with the terms of this Disclaimer should immediately cease using or referring to the Opinions. Any action by the user in connection with the information contained in the Opinions is solely at the user's discretion.

The general information contained in the Opinions is provided "as is" and without warranty of any kind, either expressed or implied. Dr. Bak Nguyen (legal name Dr. Ba Khoa Nguyen) makes every effort to ensure that the information is complete and accurate. However, there is no guarantee that the general information contained in the Opinions is always available, truthful, complete, up-to-date or relevant.

The Opinions expressed by Dr. Bak Nguyen (legal name Dr. Ba Khoa Nguyen) are personal and expressed in his own name and do not reflect the opinions of his companies, partners and other affiliates.

Dr. Bak Nguyen (legal name Dr. Ba Khoa Nguyen) also disclaims any responsibility for the content of any hyperlinks included in the Opinions.

Always seek the advice of your expert advisors, physicians or other qualified professionals with any questions you may have regarding your condition. Never disregard professional advice or delay in seeking it because of something you have read, seen or heard in the Opinions. »

## ABOUT THE AUTHOR

From Canada, **Dr. BAK NGUYEN**, Nominee Ernst and Young Entrepreneur of the year, Grand Homage Lys DIVERSITY, LinkedIn & TownHall Achiever of the year and TOP 100 Doctors 2021. Dr Bak is a cosmetic dentist, CEO and founder of Mdex & Co. His company is revolutionizing the dental field. Speaker and motivator, he wrote 72 books over 36 months accumulating many world records (to be officialized). His books are covering:

- **ENTREPRENEURSHIP**
- **LEADERSHIP**
- **QUEST OF IDENTITY**
- **DENTISTRY AND MEDICINE**
- **PARENTING**
- **CHILDREN'S BOOKS**
- **PHILOSOPHY**

In 2003, he founded Mdex, a dental company upon which in 2018, he launched the most ambitious private endeavour to reform the dental industry, Canada wide. Philosopher, he has close to his heart the quest of happiness of the people surrounding him, patients and colleagues alike. In 2020, he launched an International collaborative initiative named **THE ALPHAS** to share knowledge and for Entrepreneurs and Doctors to thrive through the Greatest Pandemic and Economic depression of our time.

In 2016, he co-found with Tranie Vo, Emotive World Incorporated, a tech research company to use technology to empower happiness and sharing. U.A.X. the ultimate audio experience is the landmark project on which the team is advancing, utilizing the technics of the movie industry and the advancement in ARTIFICIAL INTELLIGENCE to save the book industry and to upgrade the continuing education space.

These projects have allowed Dr Nguyen to attract interests from the international and diplomatic community and he is now the centre of a global discussion in the wellbeing and the future of the health profession. It is in that matter that he shares his thoughts and encourages the health community to share their own stories.

> "It's not worth it go through it alone! Together, we stand, alone, we fall."

Motivational speaker and serial entrepreneur, philosopher and author, from his own words, Dr Nguyen describes himself as a dentist by circumstances, an entrepreneur by nature and a communicator by passion.

He also holds recognitions from the Canadian Parliament and the Canadian Senate.

# SHORTCUT 1
# 408 HEALING QUOTES

by Dr BAK NGUYEN

## INTRODUCTION
BY Dr BAK NGUYEN

**PART 1**
## HEALING
Dr. BAK NGUYEN

**PART 2**
## 331 HEALING QUOTES
Dr. BAK NGUYEN

**PART 3**
## THE POWER OF QUOTES
Dr. BAK NGUYEN

**PART 4**
## 77 FAMOUS QUOTES
Dr. BAK NGUYEN

## CONCLUSION
BY Dr BAK NGUYEN

**ANNEX**
## GLOSSARY OF Dr. BAK's LIBRARY
Dr. BAK NGUYEN

# INTRODUCTION
by Dr. BAK NGUYEN

I won't lie, I am starting this book looking forward to the completion of my life's challenge writing books. I still have 13 weeks before the dateline, August 31st, 2021, to complete my next milestone world record: to write 100 books within 4 years.

I am at 90 books written so far. Okay, the **POWER OF YES** series was kind of a cheat, compiling the introduction of my books, except for the children's books, into 6 volumes. Well, what must seem like a cheat wasn't one. I learnt quickly that writing new books was much easier for me than revisiting and rewriting old ones.

So, I compiled them as I see fit. To me, those are completely new books, especially in that they are telling a whole different story. They are the story of my rise and the discovery of my powers into a Momentum.

Writing books has never been a dream nor a goal for me. It was simply a medium to express myself. 100 books later (or about to be), I have discovered ease doing so. The easy part was to let my mind free and to follow its mood and caprices.

The hard part was to find ways to captivate that energy and wild freedom into narrative and labels to keep your interests… and mine. From the outside, people are counting my titles and are mesmerized by my pace. They are even more mesmerized as they are discovering the diversity of the themes that I cover and the depth of those themes.

Oh yes, I write about my journey and reflections. But I also write about the **ENERGY FORMULA**, ways to overachieve, midlife crisis, entrepreneurship, medicine, parenting, economy, philosophy etc... I write about what I feel and understand, in that exact order.

"To write, I must feel first, and then,
I dig to understand."
Dr. Bak Nguyen

And that's how I wrote a book after the next, and the next. Within a book, finding my structure to keep pushing the narrative was the second challenge. Well, I finally found my pace as I understood the number of the Dragon, the infinite 8.

I found that wisdom writing with my son, William, as he was 8 at the time. Together, History will say that we celebrate one world record by scoring 2 more, within a month! Well, we did that discovering the power of the *number of the Dragon*: 8.

So after 16 months of writing, I started to structure my books into 8 chapters. If I have co and guest authors, the total number may change, but I try to keep mine at 8 chapters.

"At 8, the possibilities and the energy
seem to be infinite."
Dr. Bak Nguyen

That is my secret to keep pushing titles, one after the next. But there is more, how do I keep pushing my thoughts from one paragraph to the next while keeping logic and pace?

It is no secret that I started writing to prepare myself for the stage. My first public speaking event was supposed to appear and speak after the former first lady of the United States of America, Michelle Obama. Well, that never happened, but I was ready. I started writing speeches and Ted talks presentations to prepare myself.

So from the beginning, it was not about writing books but to have a dialogue with you, my audience. That's what it was, to have an audience.

Well, nowadays, our audience, whoever they are, has a very short attention span. I don't judge them, I am the same. People read headlines and zap from one channel to the next. From 45 minutes TV shows, we came to consume 4 minutes clips on YouTube, on-demand. Instagram brought that down to a minute to be featured on our feed.

No wonder why book reading is in a steep decline for the last decades. And this is where I found my talent, writing books. Well, I did so respecting the trends of today, within the attention of 60 seconds or less. And this is called a QUOTE.

Actually, a QUOTE is less than 15 seconds. Then, if you engage with your audience, they might take the next 45 seconds to process that thought and to agree or not with you. Often, they will knock their head and think: "Well said, I did not think of that one." or "That's true!"

If the older readers said that having my chapters populated with QUOTES after QUOTES somehow cut the flow of their reading, the younger audience absolutely adores that style of writing, keeping them engaged.

Well, here is my challenge: I am stuck in between. If the older audience is the one still consuming books, I am writing books what is appealing to the younger audience who do not like to read.

I did not let that stop nor slow me. I kept writing as if I was on stage, delivering speeches that kept you engaged. In other words, I entertained and inspired you. This is how I write and enjoy sharing.

And since I have a pretty short attention span myself, I keep writing with as least amount of words as possible to express an idea. Again, this is called a quote.

Because of my origin story, writing from the format of a Ted Talk, I also often write while listening to music, movie soundtracks to be more specific. Well, those have a certain pace and energy. How do I translate and incorporate into my writings? Once again, with quotes.

In the past, poets used rhymes and fixed number of syllables to pace their texts. I do not have that talent nor patience. I found another way to pace my speeches: with quotes.

After writing my 5th book and being rejected by 3 of the main national publishing companies, I got frustrated and decided that I won't be waiting nor be asking for permission. Before publishing my first book (which ended up being my 7th one, **CHANGING THE WORLD FROM A DENTAL CHAIR**), I published my writing on the walls of my clinic, using my quotes.

That brought in much attention and soul into my enterprise, **Mdex & Co**. We have people taking pictures of these quotes and publishing them on their own social media walls. We even have strangers writing back to us, asking for permission to visit and to take selfies with these quotes. Once again, quotes.

So here they are, these famous quotes, 1000 quotes from 100 of my books. I am compiling this book, **1000 Dr. BAK's QUOTES** preparing the next phase of my interaction with my audience. If writing books, combo paperback/audiobooks, and even **UAX** audiobooks (movie without image) streaming left some of them aside, I am back to my origins, pushing out QUOTES to engage with my audience, wherever they are and respecting their preferences, with QUOTES.

Quotes in a book, quotes on a mug, quotes on T-Shirt, quotes on mirrors, quotes on the wall. Maybe quotes as tattoos? I learnt a long time ago not to judge but to empower instead.

This is my take, to deliver my thoughts into a format that may serve you the way you see fit, from a QUOTE.

This is **1000 Dr. BAK's QUOTE**. Welcome to the Alphas.

Dr. BAK NGUYEN

# PART 1
## "HEALING"
by Dr. BAK NGUYEN

What was supposed to be a cheat to help me arrive at the finished line revealed itself to be a burden, a big one. I spent weeks and weeks revisiting each of my books and compiling each of my quotes into categories, 22 of them.

If I started this endeavour with the idea of cheating, my only concern was be to find enough quotes to respect my title: 1000 quotes. Well, I quickly learnt that I got it reversed! Opening my library, I found an abundance of quotes, of **pearls of wisdom**, to borrow the words of my friend and one-time co-author, Dr. Ken Serota.

And with abundance came the weight and the work. I was buried in the journey for close to 6 weeks, revisiting and compiling. I started to regret my choice. I started to panic, looking at the calendar fading away, a day after the next.

I am usually a very positive person and a very stubborn one. When I have a goal in mind, don't stand in my way! That being said, just like in each of my journeys, as I pushed forward, I learnt more about life, about myself.

If my first realization was to have a much easier time writing the next words, books, and thoughts than to recycle old ones, my second revelation was from another order, another depth. As I was compiling my quotes into categories, I was surprised by the number of quotes that I found under the theme of **HEALING**.

From book number one to book number 90, they all included healing quotes. I must tell you that this was not intentional. I wrote about what I felt and knew. I even distanced myself from one of the world's greatest motivators and speakers, Anthony Robbins, because I felt that he was more addressing broken people than empowering people to rise above themselves.

This time, I was stuck with myself, my own wording, and thoughts. With a total of 2412 quotes in the first compilation of my quotes, 331 were about healing. That's close to 14% of my library! And I never thought that I was broken to start with.

"We all need healing."
Dr. Bak Nguyen

That was my biggest realization, hacking my way into the next level. I still remember the first person who told me that I need healing, I almost sent him away. That was my first coach and mentor, Dr. Mohammed Benkhalifa.

As he was training me and preparing for power (politic), he got out of the blue, one evening, that I have to forgive myself. I did not know what he was talking about. And without reason, I became angry, answering: "What the fuck do I have to forgive myself for?!"

You have to understand that I am a very composed person. Always polite and respectful, especially to whom I respect. Dr.

Benkhalifa was amongst those people I held in high regard. So my anger and wording shocked me. He was neither surprised nor impressed.

It took me a few days to realize that with a single word, FORGIVENESS, Dr. Benkhalifa sent me on a journey that lasted many years. Today, I've learnt to always listen. Not to the words alone but to the clues and non-verbal, the *metadata*.

Anger was the truth that revealed itself that evening. I am everything but an angry man. All the people that shook my hand will tell you how joyful and cheerful I am as a person. Was that my nature or simply a coping mechanism to hide my pain and anger?

**Anger never came back to the table.**
**Frustration, maybe, but not Anger.**
**With the key of FORGIVENESS,**

**Anger became Determination.**
**Anger became Curiosity.**
**Anger became Growth.**

And so started the journey of finding my name and worth. I was still in denial, even before the facts and the clear expression of my whole being. I rarely called it healing. In my wording and mind, I twisted the concept into a positive walk, the one that heroes take: the **Quest of Identity**.

That is a very prominent theme in my writing. Now that I am breaking down my books into chapters, and my chapters into quotes, sorting them into categories, I realized that it was about healing. It all started with healing.

> "One's legend can only begin the day
> one's Quest of Identity is over."
> Dr. Bak Nguyen

Replace **Quest of Identity** with **HEALING** and it all makes so much sense! Somehow, I needed a twist of heroism to find the courage to face my demons and pain. As a doctor, I am the hero helping my patients to heal, the patient is nearly the passive passenger of the ride. I was so wrong.

> "Healing is not a destination but a journey.
> Often the first journey of your personal rise."
> Dr. Bak Nguyen

And here comes my 2413th quotes, one that will be compiled only in the next recensus, if there is a second one. But really, this is what it is, a journey.

Walking that **journey of healing**, I made the time to acknowledge what I left behind and forgotten. I will even say blacked out and blocked away. That was the cause of my anger.

But then, as I revisited my past, I released the pressure that was building up inside. Not having to contain that pressure freed much energy, now available to heal.

And that's the classic construct of our legend, to have a hero to rise above the handicaps he or she was imposed with. We don't like perfect heroes. Those we are attached to are the broken spirits who found a way to outgrow their handicaps. What does that tell you?

> "We all need healing."
> Dr. Bak Nguyen

This one is universal. Some of the pains will be inflected by a particular individual. Some of the pains by a way of life, by religion, by Conformity, by our own choices. We all have regrets and remorses.

So if you are looking to grow, your first step is to heal first. I beg you pardon, your first step is to accept that you are broken and to Dr.op the denial. Once the denial down, you will have access to much energy to start the healing process.

In my books, I called that process the **REUNIFICATION**. Only once you made peace with your past, that you are picking the pieces of yourself that you carved off that you can be whole.

"What is whole is powerful."
Dr. Bak Nguyen

That's the 2414th quote, a second one out of the current recensus. It was too powerful to leave out. If you are looking for happiness, which everyone is, heal! If you are looking for power, heal. If you are looking for abundance, heal! If you want to be a hero or even just yourself, heal!

By healing, you are whole (powerful), you are available (without anger and with much energy), you are growing (because you are now open to embrace what is out there instead of looking down on your bellybutton)

And so 1000 quotes became 2412 quotes, 22 categories, and 8 books. This is 331 healing quotes plus 77 classic Dr. Bak's quotes. Healing is important, healing is the beginning. But once that is covered, the journey ahead is as vast as the Universe.

You too, have that need, frustration, and anger. We all did it, to denial and to hideaway. Actually, being a doctor in dental surgery for 20 plus years, I learnt one important fact: you cannot force someone to heal. They have to accept the need first in order to ask and accept help.

Well, this is the healing of our souls and being, we each have our own timing and pace, no one can rush that. One can only present the key, and when we are ready, we, ourselves, will unlock our own prison.

"Because make no mistake, we are the guardians and masons of our own prison."
Dr. Bak Nguyen

And that is 2415 and 333 quotes on healing! I can't stop them from coming and I am not so far away from anger. I hope that you picked up on the trends and the metadata. Release yourself from that burden and start your journey to healing, to reunification.

The energy will be found with the dropping of your denial. The power will be within your reunification process. And the happiness will be within your new availability. We call that freedom and abundance!

This is **Shortcut volume 1, HEALING**. Welcome to the Alphas.

It all started with healing.
Heal to find your freedom.
Heal to find your powers.
Heal to be happy and whole.

**Dr. BAK NGUYEN**

# PART 2
## "331 HEALING QUOTES"
by Dr. BAK NGUYEN

## 0654

FROM LEADERSHIP, PANDORA'S BOX

" Even with scars, a healed heart is more attractive than a brand new one."

Dr. Bak Nguyen

## 0655

FROM LEADERSHIP, PANDORA'S BOX

" The Scars hold more than the memories of knowledge, and they keep the colors and the smell of emotions too."

Dr. Bak Nguyen

## 0656

FROM LEADERSHIP, PANDORA'S BOX

" The mind will etch the scars into our heart to remember, to avoid tasting the same bitterness again. Can we call that smart?"

Dr. Bak Nguyen

## 0657

FROM LEADERSHIP, PANDORA'S BOX

" I have enough from my journey to add on extra weight and pain. I don't have room to reinforce fear in my heart. "

Dr. Bak Nguyen

## 0658

FROM LEADERSHIP, PANDORA'S BOX

" Salvation is universal. Is it hope or a great lie?
The recipe is known to all, to erase
our sins before we die."

**Dr. Bak Nguyen**

## 0659

FROM LEADERSHIP, PANDORA'S BOX

" Have we really sin? Who is telling?
Worst, why are we listening?"

**Dr. Bak Nguyen**

## 0660

FROM LEADERSHIP, PANDORA'S BOX

"It will be a mistake to erase Doubt."

**Dr. Bak Nguyen**

## 0661

FROM IDENTITY, ANTHOLOGY OF QUESTS

"The ghost is still a part of life,
stuck on emotion and
thirty for one's justice."

**Dr. Bak Nguyen**

## 0662

FROM IDENTITY, ANTHOLOGY OF QUESTS

"The island of loneliness can be a cold, cold place."

**Dr. Bak Nguyen**

## 0663

FROM IDENTITY, ANTHOLOGY OF QUESTS

"Now that the victim has summoned what left of his
vitals to become a ghost, it is now rising into
a new force of nature."

**Dr. Bak Nguyen**

## 0664

FROM IDENTITY, ANTHOLOGY OF QUESTS

"In our quest for a cure, the past has much to say
but no answer to give."

**Dr. Bak Nguyen**

## 0665

FROM IDENTITY, ANTHOLOGY OF QUESTS

"Dark knights, the chords are the same,
the song can still be a happy one!"

**Dr. Bak Nguyen**

# 0666

FROM IDENTITY, ANTHOLOGY OF QUESTS

"Perfection is not ambition, it is the insecurity of one's soul to stop and starting to look back!"

Dr. Bak Nguyen

# 0667

FROM PROFESSION HEALTH

"Never be too busy to receive a feedback. Positive and negative."

Dr. Bak Nguyen

# 0668

FROM PROFESSION HEALTH

"Keep the hope high, leave both the scars and the medals in the past, since they are both death weights."

Dr. Bak Nguyen

# 0669

FROM INDUSTRIES' DISRUPTORS

"It was easier to simply not have problems!"

Dr. Bak Nguyen

# 0670

FROM AMONGST THE ALPHAS, VOLUME 2

"Healing doesn't mean to amputate
and to learn to live with less."

Dr. Bak Nguyen

# 0671

FROM AMONGST THE ALPHAS, VOLUME 2

"Dark is sadness painted, cold is regrets painted,
don't impose yours."

Dr. Bak Nguyen

# 0672

FROM AMONGST THE ALPHAS, VOLUME 2

"Anger and violence will only deepen
your pain and suffering."

Dr. Bak Nguyen

# 0673

FROM AMONGST THE ALPHAS, VOLUME 2

"Making sense and taking action have the benefit of
not leaving any free time for depression."

Dr. Bak Nguyen

## 0674

FROM AMONGST THE ALPHAS, VOLUME 2

"The day I looked up and left my bellybutton behind, that day I merged with the Universe."

**Dr. Bak Nguyen**

## 0675

FROM AMONGST THE ALPHAS, VOLUME 2

"But as I came to understand, it is either to lose them or to lose yourself!"

**Dr. Bak Nguyen**

## 0676

FROM LEADERSHIP, PANDORA'S BOX

"Sacrifices will reinforce Will, but it will also corrupt the soul with melancholy and a bitter taste, not from Life but from the lies."

**Dr. Bak Nguyen**

## 0677

FROM LEADERSHIP, PANDORA'S BOX

"Sacrifices do not always embody generosity and nobility."

**Dr. Bak Nguyen**

## 0678
FROM IDENTITY, ANTHOLOGY OF QUESTS
"Try to sing a lie, it will sound just like one!
Music is from the heart, all filters are all off!"
Dr. Bak Nguyen

## 0679
FROM IDENTITY, ANTHOLOGY OF QUESTS
"To forgive or to ignore, either way,
heal and be happy again!"
Dr. Bak Nguyen

## 0680
FROM PROFESSION HEALTH
"The freedom of choice is a burden.
Once whole, you know, you do not need
to choose anymore."
Dr. Bak Nguyen

## 0681
FROM PROFESSION HEALTH
"Once selfless, you do not need to
choose anymore, you know."
Dr. Bak Nguyen

## 0682
FROM PROFESSION HEALTH
"One's story can only begin once one's quest of identity is over. One's happiness can only be found once one's heart is whole. One's true power can only occur when one's heart is selfless and free of the burden of choices."
Dr. Bak Nguyen

## 0683
FROM PROFESSION HEALTH
"You will speak in terms of body and soul,
no more in terms of mind and heart,
leaving the body aside any longer."
Dr. Bak Nguyen

## 0684
FROM PROFESSION HEALTH
"Don't expect the Gratitude from the same source that needed your help."
Dr. Bak Nguyen

## 0685
FROM PROFESSION HEALTH
"You can believe in something or someone and make it happen. Or you can test everything
and rewrite the past."
Dr. Bak Nguyen

## 0686

FROM PROFESSION HEALTH

"Once we accept recognition, only then,
we can show gratitude in return.
Before, it was an unknown variable."

Dr. Bak Nguyen

## 0687

FROM PROFESSION HEALTH

"Forgive and forget, embrace and hope!"

Dr. Bak Nguyen

## 0688

FROM PROFESSION HEALTH

"I embraced the liability
and made it my strength."

Dr. Bak Nguyen

## 0689

FROM PROFESSION HEALTH

"To believe is the first step to win, to heal."

Dr. Bak Nguyen

## 0690

FROM INDUSTRIES' DISRUPTORS

"I did my time in, now it's my time to fly high! "

Dr. Bak Nguyen

## 0691
FROM INDUSTRIES' DISRUPTORS

"As human beings, we have the bad habit of trying
to attach everything down, thinking that
it will last forever."
**Dr. Bak Nguyen**


## 0692
FROM INDUSTRIES' DISRUPTORS

"Our kind is deeply rooted in fear."
**Dr. Bak Nguyen**


## 0693
FROM INDUSTRIES' DISRUPTORS

"The only one that you keep sleeping with is yourself,
night after night. Learn to appreciate that person."
**Dr. Bak Nguyen**


## 0694
FROM THE POWER BEHIND THE ALPHA

" Perfection is a lie. Aim for harmony."
**Dr. Bak Nguyen**


## 0695
FROM THE POWER BEHIND THE ALPHA

"To be happy, one must heal first."
**Dr. Bak Nguyen**

## 0696

FROM THE POWER BEHIND THE ALPHA

"To forgive is to understand deeply the other party,
to walk in their shoes and to restrain
ourselves from judging."
Dr. Bak Nguyen

## 0697

FROM MOMENTUM TRANSFER

" Harder than to find yourself,
is to accept what you've found! "
Dr. Bak Nguyen

## 0698

FROM MOMENTUM TRANSFER

" Find your own voice and nurture it into harmony.
Harmony, not perfection."
Dr. Bak Nguyen

## 0699

FROM MOMENTUM TRANSFER

" Do not look for perfection, look for harmony."
Dr. Bak Nguyen

## 0700

FROM MOMENTUM TRANSFER

"Being whole is to accept who you are
for all the facets of your being."

Dr. Bak Nguyen

## 0701

FROM MOMENTUM TRANSFER

"To heal does not mean to erase the scars
but to accept what was and to move forward."

Dr. Bak Nguyen

## 0702

FROM MOMENTUM TRANSFER

"A bonsai is no art, it is pure pride,
the arrogance to think that we can outsmart nature."

Dr. Bak Nguyen

## 0703

FROM MOMENTUM TRANSFER

"Forgive yourself. You have
to forgive yourself and to let go."

Dr. Bak Nguyen

## 0704

FROM HYBRID

"Healing from conformity.
Healing with continuity."

Dr. Bak Nguyen

## 0705

FROM HYBRID

"Nor Anger nor Rage are the answers.
They might be natural reactions,
but not answers."

Dr. Bak Nguyen

## 0706

FROM HYBRID

"Your quest of identity is to heal and to find peace."

Dr. Bak Nguyen

## 0707

FROM HYBRID

"Seeing the whole picture, you'll realize
that you're a part of the problem.
Only then, you'll stop judging
yourself."

Dr. Bak Nguyen

## 0708
"Hope is the hunger of tomorrow
with the determination of today."
Dr. Bak Nguyen

## 0709
"I was both of them, bearing the liability of both of
them. That's the hybrid that Conformity
and Society made of me."
Dr. Bak Nguyen

## 0710
"Fear has its own way of turning time
into time-loop..."
Dr. Bak Nguyen

## 0711
"The burden is just compiling with each day spent
under the shadow of doubt and fear."
Dr. Bak Nguyen

## 0712
FROM HYBRID

"To know and to fear is the worst paralysis.
It is frustration."

**Dr. Bak Nguyen**

## 0713
FROM HYBRID

"Jealousy and Insecurity are pure poisons.
Be aware."

**Dr. Bak Nguyen**

## 0714
FROM REBOOT, TO GROW FROM MIDLIFE CRISIS

"There is something wrong from the fabric
if we have to recall so many of those!"

**Dr. Bak Nguyen**

## 0715
FROM REBOOT, TO GROW FROM MIDLIFE CRISIS

"Love and happiness are living concepts.
They grow and evolve, so should we."

**Dr. Bak Nguyen**

## 0716

"To have our natural desire suddenly cut out from us,
they gave it a name, evil."

Dr. Bak Nguyen

## 0717

"Nature intended for us to be hungry for food,
for security and for sex."

Dr. Bak Nguyen

## 0718

"A wedding is like something we need to do
just not to miss out on life, on love."

Dr. Bak Nguyen

## 0719

"For my sake, the sake of those I love,
I give up on Pride. Instead, I now keep
my heart and head open to adapt."

Dr. Bak Nguyen

## 0720
"Don't throw anything through the window just yet.
Play it cool and keep the communication
truthful and respectful."
Dr. Bak Nguyen

## 0721
"The biggest problem one face
is when one is in denial."
Dr. Bak Nguyen

## 0722
"Everything we created, we can also fix! "
Dr. Bak Nguyen

## 0723
"The problem starts to occur as we did it
in the name of Love, with God as witness."
Dr. Bak Nguyen

## 0724

"From a business point of view,
stop fearing and start celebrating!"
Dr. Bak Nguyen

## 0725

"We are on the wrong side of the track since
Mother nature will always know more
and better than us."
Dr. Bak Nguyen

## 0726

"One way in, one way out, Pain and Pride."
Dr. Bak Nguyen

## 0727

"To stay calm, do not feed on the frenzy.
Like any storm, it will pass."
Dr. Bak Nguyen

## 0728

"To face the Tornado is suicide! Don't go for a Face Off with Jealousy, thinking that you can win."

Dr. Bak Nguyen

## 0729

"The Whole is what we are.
Not what we have."

Dr. Bak Nguyen

## 0730

"We are everything, we do not possess anything."

Dr. Bak Nguyen

## 0731

"MidLife Crisis is the chance to release the weaknesses and lies to rebuild with more strengths and flexibility."

Dr. Bak Nguyen

## 0732
"To this bad situation, there are even worst answers,
Guilt and Blame."
Dr. Bak Nguyen

## 0733
"Some will fall in love with their own wounds
looking at them for too long, too closely."
Dr. Bak Nguyen

## 0734
"Pain does not have to be as great as Love
to prove that Love was real."
Dr. Bak Nguyen

## 0735
"Pick up the pieces and start rebuilding, not blaming."
Dr. Bak Nguyen

## 0736
"As soon as possible, find Hope, once more."
Dr. Bak Nguyen

## 0737

"To fight melancholy and depression, use fear to keep moving until the pain and Anger completely fade away."

Dr. Bak Nguyen

## 0738

"Rebuild with Gratitude and Flexibility."

Dr. Bak Nguyen

## 0739

"The more joins there are, the more flexibility we get."

Dr. Bak Nguyen

## 0740

"I am it all. Not I have, nor I want it all."

Dr. Bak Nguyen

## 0741

"We like and hate what we are, through our ears and eyes, the filter is permanent, us."

Dr. Bak Nguyen

## 0742

"The intent was to connect,
the result is to help ease their pain."
Dr. Bak Nguyen

## 0743

"Trust what you feel more than what you hear."
Dr. Bak Nguyen

## 0744

"Words are powerful since they program
your core beliefs"
Dr. Bak Nguyen

## 0745

"I prefer Hope to Fear, every single time."
Dr. Bak Nguyen

## 0746

"Sad and true are the damages of negativity
on one soul."
Dr. Bak Nguyen

## 0747

FROM LEVERAGE COMMUNICATION INTO SUCCESS

"Eventually, you become what you say you are."

Dr. Bak Nguyen

## 0748

FROM LEVERAGE COMMUNICATION INTO SUCCESS

"Find your worth in the service of others
and the label won't matter anymore."

Dr. Bak Nguyen

## 0749

FROM FORCES OF NATURE

"I am not perfect, they are not perfect.
Let's leave it at that."

Dr. Bak Nguyen

## 0750

FROM FORCES OF NATURE

"I stop letting people judge me with their opinions,
even with love, they all have their boundaries."

Dr. Bak Nguyen

## 0751

FROM FORCES OF NATURE

"I try to love first and if that is not working,
then, I ignore."

**Dr. Bak Nguyen**

## 0752

FROM FORCES OF NATURE

"Inertia was not to stand still but to find the strength
to deal with multiple opposites and to keep balance."

**Dr. Bak Nguyen**

## 0752

FROM FORCES OF NATURE

"The past got me the potential to write the future."

**Dr. Bak Nguyen**

## 0753

FROM FORCES OF NATURE

"To beat Myopia, go fast!
You'll be amazed how far you can get."

**Dr. Bak Nguyen**

## 0754
FROM FORCES OF NATURE
"Myopia got the best of me, trapping me
in my own armour, my own success."
Dr. Bak Nguyen

## 0755
FROM FORCES OF NATURE
"Demon and angel are two and one
at the same time."
Dr. Bak Nguyen

## 0756
FROM FORCES OF NATURE
"Not all truths are useful.
One must stand ready first."
Dr. Bak Nguyen

## 0757
FROM FORCES OF NATURE
"Staring in the eyes of truth for too long
will change your heart into a heart of stone."
Dr. Bak Nguyen

## 0758
FROM FORCES OF NATURE
"Truth is the cold and divine reflection
of what and who we are."
Dr. Bak Nguyen

## 0759

"The shield of pride is the only weapon of use
in front of truth, the angel."

Dr. Bak Nguyen

## 0760

"One cannot kill a force of nature.
One simply must grow into one
to stop the threats."

Dr. Bak Nguyen

## 0761

"Truth may not be pretty but it is no devil."

Dr. Bak Nguyen

## 0762

"In order for one to believe, there must be no doubt,
therefore, no but. "

Dr. Bak Nguyen

## 0763

"No one can be powerful by himself.
Imagine half of him... what chance does he has? "

Dr. Bak Nguyen

## 0764

FROM FORCES OF NATURE

"After the healing, once whole,
all there are, are choices."

Dr. Bak Nguyen

## 0765

FROM FORCES OF NATURE

"There is no bigger foe than the one within."

Dr. Bak Nguyen

## 0766

FROM FORCES OF NATURE

" Domestication is an unnatural and cruel process."

Dr. Bak Nguyen

## 0767

FROM FORCES OF NATURE

"It's crazy how we can be our greatest enemy."

Dr. Bak Nguyen

## 0768

FROM FORCES OF NATURE

"Few will heal completely from the infection of
expectation. For the rest of their lives,
they might be chasing ghosts."

Dr. Bak Nguyen

## 0769
FROM FORCES OF NATURE
"It was done in good faith, but with such ignorance then. So it is with the virus of expectation today, in good faith but with such ignorance still."
Dr. Bak Nguyen

## 0770
FROM FORCES OF NATURE
"To kill a mind, get it to think in poor ways: to divide and subtract."
Dr. Bak Nguyen

## 0771
FROM FORCES OF NATURE
"Intimidation is not the recognition of the strength of one but rather the littleness of the other."
Dr. Bak Nguyen

## 0772
FROM FORCES OF NATURE
"Myopia has always been there, it has always cared. If the sight is blurry, one just needs to choose to clear his eyes from the oil."
Dr. Bak Nguyen

## 0773
### FROM FORCES OF NATURE
"We have come to know each other well enough to laugh together, not at each other…"
Dr. Bak Nguyen

## 0774
### FROM SELFMADE
"Chains are not roots, nothing is written in stone. And since the universe is expanding and alive. however they put it, nothing will last forever."
Dr. Bak Nguyen

## 0775
### FROM SELFMADE
"I changed my frustration into excitement, most of the time."
Dr. Bak Nguyen

## 0776
### FROM SELFMADE
"To fall is not to fail."
Dr. Bak Nguyen

## 0777
### FROM SELFMADE
"There is simply no wisdom to learn from someone who never did."
Dr. Bak Nguyen

## 0778

FROM SELFMADE

"I still have to survive emotionally
through the process."

**Dr. Bak Nguyen**

## 0779

FROM SELFMADE

"However old you are, now is the time,
you can't change the past but you can
choose your future."

**Dr. Bak Nguyen**

## 0780

FROM SELFMADE

"I refuse to average my intelligence and my passion
just for the sake of loyalty and averaging."

**Dr. Bak Nguyen**

## 0781

FROM SELFMADE

"I can't change the past,
but I can surely build the future."

**Dr. Bak Nguyen**

## 0782

FROM SELFMADE

"I changed and money started flowing in.
Not the other way around."

Dr. Bak Nguyen

## 0783

FROM SELFMADE

"Don't run from your emotions.
They are from your heart, and our heart
is bigger than your brain."

Dr. Bak Nguyen

## 0784

FROM SELFMADE

"Carve out your heart and throw it away.
Sounded stupid? And yet that's what
we are trained to do."

Dr. Bak Nguyen

## 0785

FROM SELFMADE

"Give yourself the time
and space to be."

Dr. Bak Nguyen

## 0786

FROM SELFMADE

"The longer you look at something,
the more perspective it will gain. You and Time are
what giving perspective to things,
events, and people."

Dr. Bak Nguyen


## 0787

FROM CHAMPION MINDSET

"Learning to heal and to keep being true
to myself was the most valuable thing
I've learnt on my journey."

Dr. Bak Nguyen


## 0788

FROM CHAMPION MINDSET

"We are what we feel."

Dr. Bak Nguyen


## 0789

FROM CHAMPION MINDSET

"At the end of the day,
the sun will rise again, ahead."

Dr. Bak Nguyen

## 0790

"With hope, with respect, with dignity, everything is possible!"

**Dr. Bak Nguyen**

## 0791

"What can be a liability can also be seen as an asset and be leveraged as an opportunity."

**Dr. Bak Nguyen**

## 0792

"Oh yes, procrastination and doubt will kill many, many potentials."

**Dr. Bak Nguyen**

## 0793

"Eventually, you will make a flight out of your fall."

**Dr. Bak Nguyen**

## 0794

"The real enemy is always from within."

**Dr. Bak Nguyen**

## 0795

FROM CHAMPION MINDSET

"There is a price for everything."

**Dr. Bak Nguyen**

## 0796

FROM HOW TO WRITE A BOOK IN 30 DAYS

"To feel is often hard and costly.
Emotions can be wild!"

**Dr. Bak Nguyen**

## 0797

FROM HOW TO WRITE A BOOK IN 30 DAYS

"The secret is within one word: feelings."

**Dr. Bak Nguyen**

## 0798

FROM HOW TO WRITE A BOOK IN 30 DAYS

"Artists don't erase; they paint on top of what was."

**Dr. Bak Nguyen**

## 0799

FROM HOW TO WRITE A BOOK IN 30 DAYS

"Emotions are what's colouring
all the facts in our lives."

**Dr. Bak Nguyen**

## 0800
FROM THE BOOK OF LEGENDS, VOLUME 2
"It is called the path to redemption,
to make up for your mistakes."
Dr. Bak Nguyen

## 0801
FROM THE BOOK OF LEGENDS, VOLUME 2
"A rock feels nothing but
coldness and loneliness for eternity."
Dr. Bak Nguyen

## 0802
FROM THE BOOK OF LEGENDS, VOLUME 2
"Oh yes, you have to learn to receive too."
Dr. Bak Nguyen

## 0803
FROM THE BOOK OF LEGENDS, VOLUME 2
"Your heart deserves more than coldness."
Dr. Bak Nguyen

## 0804
FROM THE BOOK OF LEGENDS, VOLUME 2
"Talking is not always helping,
even if what you are saying is the truth."
Dr. Bak Nguyen

## 0805

FROM POWER, EMOTIONAL INTELLIGENCE

"I've finally aligned my emotions and my ambitions.
With that, my wings grew back."

Dr. Bak Nguyen

## 0806

FROM POWER, EMOTIONAL INTELLIGENCE

"To be in HARMONY is to be at peace with oneself."

Dr. Bak Nguyen

## 0807

FROM POWER, EMOTIONAL INTELLIGENCE

"Emotions can raise walls or calm the storm.
It's up to you to stir them."

Dr. Bak Nguyen

## 0808

FROM BRANDING

"Adjectives are what amplify or minimize a fact.
Play it wisely."

Dr. Bak Nguyen

## 0809

FROM BRANDING

"Good or bad, let it out! If you don't what's ever left
inside will rot and corrupt everything it touches."

Dr. Bak Nguyen

## 0810

FROM BRANDING

"I created most of my problems,
and from my own creations, I found
the solution to each one of them…
or almost."

Dr. Bak Nguyen

## 0811

FROM BRANDING

"I was strong before,
now I am light and even stronger."

Dr. Bak Nguyen

## 0812

FROM HORIZON VOLUME TWO

"There are no perfect identity nor perfect choices,
just who we are and what we do with it."

Dr. Bak Nguyen

## 0813

FROM HORIZON VOLUME TWO

"It's hard to learn when you do not see the truth."

Dr. Bak Nguyen

## 0814

FROM THE POWER OF YES VOLUME 3

"Openness and respect are what I've gained saying yes by default."

Dr. Bak Nguyen

## 0815

FROM THE POWER OF YES VOLUME 3

"I do not believe in perfection, I believe in the flow, the fluidity."

Dr. Bak Nguyen

## 0816

FROM HOW TO NOT FAIL AS A DENTIST

"Perfection is a lie, Time is all you hold true."

Dr. Bak Nguyen

## 0817

FROM HOW TO WRITE A SUCCESSFUL BUSINESS PLAN

"To treat complacency, amputation is often the only remedy..."

Dr. Bak Nguyen

## 0818

"Never relinquish your judgement
to anyone but your heart."

**Dr. Bak Nguyen**

## 0819

"Choose wisely whom you are sharing your temple
with, since that can undo your temple in an instant."

**Dr. Bak Nguyen**

## 0820

"Too often, a Castle is a liability."

**Dr. Bak Nguyen**

## 0821

"A Castle is a House, not a home."

**Dr. Bak Nguyen**

## 0822

"Don't rush into something just to fail."

**Dr. Bak Nguyen**

## 0823

FROM MINDSET ARMORY

"Jealousy has an ugly face, everyone knows that.
But why so many embrace it?"

Dr. Bak Nguyen

## 0824

FROM MINDSET ARMORY

"Jealousy doesn't like the light since it is shadow."

Dr. Bak Nguyen

## 0825

FROM HUMILITY FOR SUCCESS

"They grew roots thinking that it will stabilize them
and ease their pain..."

Dr. Bak Nguyen

## 0826

FROM HUMILITY FOR SUCCESS

"Momentum can be a force that will stabilize
your senses and bring you comfort."

Dr. Bak Nguyen

## 0827

"Those past medals can be dead weight
if one is stuck on or in them."

Dr. Bak Nguyen

## 0828

"No Gratitude, no Humility, but Pride here."

Dr. Bak Nguyen

## 0829

"To come back from the cold
is one of the ultimate tests of character."

Dr. Bak Nguyen

## 0830

"Once you know who you are,
your past does not define you anymore."

Dr. Bak Nguyen

## 0831

FROM HUMILITY FOR SUCCESS

"Do yourself a favour and write that down:
Perfection is a lie."

**Dr. Bak Nguyen**

## 0832

FROM HUMILITY FOR SUCCESS

"Peers are simply another word for foe, in disguise."

**Dr. Bak Nguyen**

## 0833

FROM HUMILITY FOR SUCCESS

"To make it real, don't say it, don't write it, feel it.
And to feel, one must walk."

**Dr. Bak Nguyen**

## 0834

FROM MASTERMIND

"Being genuine is the kindest
of attitude toward ourselves."

**Dr. Bak Nguyen**

## 0835
FROM MASTERMIND

"Your name was given, now it is time for you
to give it its worth."
Dr. Bak Nguyen

## 0836
FROM MASTERMIND

"I believe in the balance of the Universe.
I am a little part of the Universe, little inside of a much
greater scheme. So I am not balance itself."
Dr. Bak Nguyen

## 0837
FROM MASTERMIND

"You attract what you are."
Dr. Bak Nguyen

## 0838
FROM MASTERMIND

"Opinions are cheap, feedbacks are opinions.
Testimonials, on the other hand, require commitment.
And commitment, I can relate to."
Dr. Bak Nguyen

## 0839

FROM MASTERMIND

"Everything outside of my power,
I simply do not care!"

Dr. Bak Nguyen

## 0840

FROM MASTERMIND

"What you feel and how you see yourself
are the keys to your success."

Dr. Bak Nguyen

## 0841

FROM THE ENERGY FORMULA

"Ever seen Michael Phelps swim with his medals?"

Dr. Bak Nguyen

## 0842

FROM THE ENERGY FORMULA

"There is nothing natural about GUILT.
It is simply a clever way to castrate one."

Dr. Bak Nguyen

## 0843

FROM THE ENERGY FORMULA

"The Quest of Identity is mostly a lonely path.
Everyone has to walk it, but no one can do
this one with you."

Dr. Bak Nguyen

## 0844
FROM THE ENERGY FORMULA
"Every time you doubt yourself, it is not your Identity that you are doubting, but your Confidence."
### Dr. Bak Nguyen

## 0845
FROM THE ENERGY FORMULA
"Perfection is a lie. Aim for Harmony instead."
### Dr. Bak Nguyen

## 0846
FROM THE ENERGY FORMULA
"There is no such thing as bad Energy."
### Dr. Bak Nguyen

## 0847
FROM THE ENERGY FORMULA
"Speed, Momentum and resilience are the keys to break the downward spiral."
### Dr. Bak Nguyen

## 0848
FROM THE ENERGY FORMULA
"The flow of life is moving. You can either let go and follow, dive and discover, even swim against it to train. The arrogance is to think that you can stop it, standing still."
### Dr. Bak Nguyen

## 0849
FROM THE ENERGY FORMULA
"To HAVE is trivial. To BE is overrated.
To MATTER is happiness."
**Dr. Bak Nguyen**

## 0850
FROM THE ENERGY FORMULA
"It is each one's choice to see to feel
and to act, or not."
**Dr. Bak Nguyen**

## 0851
FROM THE ENERGY FORMULA
"Harmony is your way to be one with nature.
Therefore, abstract the friction."
**Dr. Bak Nguyen**

## 0852
FROM THE ENERGY FORMULA
"Be one with the Universe,
and the Universe won't resist you."
**Dr. Bak Nguyen**

## 0853
FROM THE ENERGY FORMULA
"Your Identity is a label pending at your neck.
Will it be written on paper, forged in metal or
sculpted in the rock, it is your choice.
It is you that will wear it every minute of every day. "

**Dr. Bak Nguyen**

## 0854
FROM THE ENERGY FORMULA
"Fool your own Identity and the way you see yourself,
and you will become so much more. "

**Dr. Bak Nguyen**

## 0855
FROM PLAYBOOK INTRODUCTION VOLUME 1
"Jealousy has an ugly head."

**Dr. Bak Nguyen**

## 0856
FROM PLAYBOOK INTRODUCTION VOLUME 1
"Well, their fear, even if it was from love, will poke
holes into your confidence, ensuring your doom,
out of love!"

**Dr. Bak Nguyen**

## 0857

FROM PLAYBOOK INTRODUCTION VOLUME 1

"Love, accept it gratefully and gracefully.
Doubts and fears stay as far as those as possible.
You have enough dealing with your own."

Dr. Bak Nguyen

## 0858

FROM PLAYBOOK INTRODUCTION VOLUME 1

"Start with your heart and your head will follow."

Dr. Bak Nguyen

## 0859

FROM PLAYBOOK INTRODUCTION VOLUME 1

"We are all looking for energy, all the time."

Dr. Bak Nguyen

## 0860

FROM PLAYBOOK INTRODUCTION VOLUME 2

"Don't try to be a millionaire within a crowd of small-minded people. You will never rise. If you do, after years of misery, there will take you apart limb by limb."

Dr. Bak Nguyen

## 0861

FROM PLAYBOOK INTRODUCTION VOLUME 2

"They called it to be smart, I called it judging."

Dr. Bak Nguyen

## 0862

FROM PLAYBOOK INTRODUCTION VOLUME 2

"The drama, sure, but the pain, not so much."

Dr. Bak Nguyen

## 0863

FROM PLAYBOOK INTRODUCTION VOLUME 2

"The negative and critics are always the loudest
sounds in the background. Stay far enough,
and they will sound like cheering!"

Dr. Bak Nguyen

## 0864

FROM SUCCESS IS A CHOICE

"To find an equilibrium is to accept the situation as is
and to find a way to cope with it. "

Dr. Bak Nguyen

## 0865

FROM SUCCESS IS A CHOICE

"From the pain, I found leverage to outset
my laziness and complacency."

Dr. Bak Nguyen

## 0866

FROM SUCCESS IS A CHOICE

"In every pain, there is either defeat or leverage."

Dr. Bak Nguyen

## 0867

"Be open to embrace the new
if you want a change in your life."
Dr. Bak Nguyen

## 0868

"We all have our weakness. I leverage mine!"
Dr. Bak Nguyen

## 0869

"Being polite and fitting in are not always helping,
especially when you are trying to break bad habits."
Dr. Bak Nguyen

## 0870

"We really are the sum of all of our decisions
and the accumulation of its consequences."
Dr. Bak Nguyen

# 0871

FROM THE 90 DAYS CHALLENGE

"To fit in is a core training most of us
received since birth."
**Dr. Bak Nguyen**

# 0872

FROM THE 90 DAYS CHALLENGE

"Weight and health are the consequences of our
lifestyle and by default settings."
**Dr. Bak Nguyen**

# 0873

FROM THE 90 DAYS CHALLENGE

"The success of a life change is based, not motivation
and will power alone, but on awareness and fun.
That's the only way to make any change last.
Lasting is the key to success."
**Dr. Bak Nguyen**

# 0874

FROM THE 90 DAYS CHALLENGE

"You have to believe that it is possible
and then, not make a big deal out of it,
to increment lasting results."
**Dr. Bak Nguyen**

## 0875

FROM THE 90 DAYS CHALLENGE

"To stop and stare never led anywhere."

**Dr. Bak Nguyen**

## 0876

FROM THE 90 DAYS CHALLENGE

"We are what we believe."

**Dr. Bak Nguyen**

## 0877

FROM RISING

"You want to rise, drop the lies and the fears."

**Dr. Bak Nguyen**

## 0878

FROM RISING

"To sail, one has to either cut or pull up the anchor."

**Dr. Bak Nguyen**

## 0879

FROM RISING

"If you want control, don't play the victim, ever."

**Dr. Bak Nguyen**

## 0880

FROM RISING

"Fighting is not the only way to victory,
just the choice by default."

Dr. Bak Nguyen

## 0881

FROM RISING

"Have your head to serve your heart,
never the another way around."

Dr. Bak Nguyen

## 0882

FROM RISING

"The day I rose was the day hope outgrew fear."

Dr. Bak Nguyen

## 0883

FROM RISING

"Hope is in your heart, Fear, in your mind."

Dr. Bak Nguyen

## 0884

FROM RISING

"Look up if you want to rise up.
Looking down won't get you where you want to go."

Dr. Bak Nguyen

## 0885
FROM RISING

"To rise up, I let go of control, most if not all of it!"
Dr. Bak Nguyen

## 0886
FROM RISING

"Freedom is the absence of control."
Dr. Bak Nguyen

## 0887
FROM RISING

"We all make our own hell. Some calls it home, some calls it boundary, others will choose to call them values. No matter the label, they are all responsible for the scarcity in your life."
Dr. Bak Nguyen

## 0888
FROM RISING

"Yes, each scar has its story, don't forget those. Although they are not a map, there are your stripes."
Dr. Bak Nguyen

## 0889
"Nothing is set in stone, put that through your head, the sooner, the less painful your journey will be!"
Dr. Bak Nguyen

## 0890
"Lying, you are fooling yourself and are cutting yourself from most of the universal laws. Believe and leverage instead."
Dr. Bak Nguyen

## 0891
"Do your best and trust the universe to react to you."
Dr. Bak Nguyen

## 0892
"Make leverage out of each of your liability to thrive. Survival isn't the only option."
Dr. Bak Nguyen

## 0893

"Adapt or disappear, this is your choice."

**Dr. Bak Nguyen**

## 0894

FROM AFTERMATH

"I did not create the storm, I can still surf it."

**Dr. Bak Nguyen**

## 0895

FROM RELEVANCY

"We are what we are. We are what we choose.
There is little more one can do,
but so much one can choose."

**Dr. Bak Nguyen**

## 0896

FROM RELEVANCY

"I reinvented myself at each turn,
leaving burdens and medals behind."

**Dr. Bak Nguyen**

## 0897

FROM RELEVANCY

"The best prisons are the one you polished
with your tongue and affection."
Dr. Bak Nguyen


## 0898

FROM RELEVANCY

"To counterbalance your urge for perfection,
look at the alternatives."
Dr. Bak Nguyen


## 0899

FROM RELEVANCY

"The skills are within, the subject is ahead,
in front of you."
Dr. Bak Nguyen


## 0900

FROM RELEVANCY

"Since it is not true,
perfection is pure pride!"
Dr. Bak Nguyen

## 0901

FROM RELEVANCY

"In the COVID war, Time is not the answer, Speed is.
Speed, Humility and Flexibility."

**Dr. Bak Nguyen**

## 0902

FROM RELEVANCY

"Bigger the pain, bigger the fear,
bigger the intolerance."

**Dr. Bak Nguyen**

## 0903

FROM RELEVANCY

"Dialoguing is the first step to relevancy."

**Dr. Bak Nguyen**

## 0904

FROM MIDAS TOUCH

"To spoil yourself is the best way to keep
an open mind on what is to come!"

**Dr. Bak Nguyen**

## 0905
FROM MIDAS TOUCH
"Insecurity, like moisture, can only exist where there is shadow. Not within the light of the sun!"
Dr. Bak Nguyen

## 0906
FROM MIDAS TOUCH
"To be selfless, one needs to be whole first."
Dr. Bak Nguyen

## 0907
FROM MIDAS TOUCH
"Pain is physical, fear is mental."
Dr. Bak Nguyen

## 0908
FROM MIDAS TOUCH
"Being whole will lead to selflessness. Selflessness will lead to lightness and lightness is speed!"
Dr. Bak Nguyen

## 0909
FROM MIDAS TOUCH
"Hope is your best ally, always."
Dr. Bak Nguyen

## 0910
### FROM MIDAS TOUCH
"Don't judge anyone,
even if you think you know."
**Dr. Bak Nguyen**


## 0911
### FROM MIDAS TOUCH
"Once in a while, we can truly connect
with another soul and dance in synergy."
**Dr. Bak Nguyen**


## 0912
### FROM MIDAS TOUCH
"Words from an honest heart
will revive and grow you."
**Dr. Bak Nguyen**


## 0913
### FROM THE POWER OF Dr.
"Good and bad, I had, I did.
I wrote and shared, and I moved on."
**Dr. Bak Nguyen**

## 0914
"Healing will come from hope.
And hope can only spread as we connect.
That's the power of PEER-2-PEER."
Dr. Bak Nguyen

## 0915
FROM TORNADO
"I found my speed running away from my demons.
Then, I leveraged my demons, doubling down on
them to increase my speed."
Dr. Bak Nguyen

## 0916
FROM TORNADO
"Regrets and doubts are siblings."
Dr. Bak Nguyen

## 0917
FROM TORNADO
"Writing is not about the wording, but the narrative.
Everyone has a story to tell."
Dr. Bak Nguyen

## 0918
FROM HORIZON VOLUME THREE
"Fear is not just an emotion. Fear is also followed by some of the most powerful hormones: cortisol."
Dr. Bak Nguyen

## 0919
FROM HORIZON VOLUME THREE
"Be genuine and share openly.
That's your way to freedom."
Dr. Bak Nguyen

## 0920
FROM HORIZON VOLUME THREE
"The more I open, the faster I grow.
This is no mindset, it is a habit."
Dr. Bak Nguyen

## 0921
FROM HORIZON VOLUME THREE
"Open your mind to grow.
Then, to keep growing, open your heart.
Then do it all over again to have fun."
Dr. Bak Nguyen

## 0922
FROM HORIZON VOLUME THREE
"To do and to keep doing, one must feel."
**Dr. Bak Nguyen**

## 0923
FROM EMPOWERMENT
"From my wounds and my pride, I learnt.
To build, look for a partner, someone with
different views and experiences."
**Dr. Bak Nguyen**

## 0924
FROM EMPOWERMENT
"While I empower others,
Hope empowers me while
Love healed me."
**Dr. Bak Nguyen**

## 0925
FROM EMPOWERMENT
"One word, forgiveness, opened my heart."
**Dr. Bak Nguyen**

## 0926

FROM EMPOWERMENT

"The minute expectations set in, Hope will fade."

**Dr. Bak Nguyen**

## 0927

FROM EMPOWERMENT

"Exclusivity, fidelity, forever, sacrifice,
those aren't words, but worms."

**Dr. Bak Nguyen**

## 0928

FROM EMPOWERMENT

"You are energy. Share and your energy
will expand. That's growth."

**Dr. Bak Nguyen**

## 0929

FROM THE MODERN WOMAN

"There is no remedy to healing in the past..."

**Dr. Bak Nguyen**

## 0930
FROM THE MODERN WOMAN
"We've all received different trades and assets from God. Use them, use them not, that is your choice and mindset. Whatever you decide, you will be walking its consequences."
Dr. Bak Nguyen

## 0931
FROM BOOTCAMP
"Habits die hard. Mindsets are much more stubborn than habits."
Dr. Bak Nguyen

## 0932
FROM THE UAX STORY
"Doubt lays in the head. Fear lays in the heart. Hormones are from the body."
Dr. Bak Nguyen

## 0933
FROM THE UAX STORY
"Every time we feel, we open up. That's how the message can get through."
Dr. Bak Nguyen

## 0934

"I was at the doors of Hollywood, and I traded in my
Speed and Power for a dental licence
and the pace of Conformity!"

**Dr. Bak Nguyen**

## 0935

"What started as a curse became a blessing,
because I kept pushing to find leverage."

**Dr. Bak Nguyen**

## 0936

"At the end of each journey, a new one awaits."

**Dr. Bak Nguyen**

## 0937

FROM TOUCHSTONE, LEVERAGING TODAY'S PSYCHOLOGICAL SMOG

"Fighting our body will simply be a waste of energy.
Accepting it will give us an edge."

**Dr. Bak Nguyen**

# 0938

"Just like your hormones, there is no half response.
Don't amputate, embrace fully."

Dr. Bak Nguyen

# 0939

"The day I emptied my heart of all the burdens,
that day, success, joy, and friendship came to me.
They've been my companions ever since."

Dr. Bak Nguyen

# 0940

"Hope is not something to be found, but something
to be heard. Hope is that little voice inside of our
heart as we wake up every morning."

Dr. Bak Nguyen

# 0941

"I dictate my own terms. That's how I transpose
Pressure into Tension."

Dr. Bak Nguyen

## 0942
"Others call that meditation,
I simply call it my next book."
**Dr. Bak Nguyen**

## 0943
"Nothing drilled in by an exterior force will last
forever. Nature has its ways to resume its course.
It is called Time."
**Dr. Bak Nguyen**

## 0944
"There is something very concise with emotions,
they never go away."
**Dr. Bak Nguyen**

## 0945
"I rather have the scar than to give it my life."
**Dr. Bak Nguyen**

## 0946

FROM TOUCHSTONE, LEVERAGING TODAY'S PSYCHOLOGICAL SMOG

"Morale, hope and actions are the best remedies to stress and its accumulation. "

**Dr. Bak Nguyen**

## 0947

FROM TOUCHSTONE, LEVERAGING TODAY'S PSYCHOLOGICAL SMOG

"Stay away from fear and stress is almost gone!"

**Dr. Bak Nguyen**

## 0948

FROM TOUCHSTONE, LEVERAGING TODAY'S PSYCHOLOGICAL SMOG

"If you want a sure keystone to defeat stress, look for fun."

**Dr. Bak Nguyen**

## 0949

FROM ALPHA LADDERS VOLUME ONE

"This journey cannot be forced, but when the time comes, you'll know and will walk without fear. Much hesitation, but not fear."

**Dr. Bak Nguyen**

# 0950

FROM ALPHA LADDERS VOLUME ONE

"Emotions are the signatures of a moment."

Dr. Bak Nguyen

# 0951

FROM ALPHA LADDERS VOLUME ONE

"I stop trying to duplicate what I hear,
I simply dance along."

Dr. Bak Nguyen

# 0952

FROM ALPHA LADDERS VOLUME ONE

"Freeing your emotions is how one empties him or
herself to vibrate at a higher frequency."

Dr. Bak Nguyen

# 0953

FROM THE RISE OF THE UNICORN VOLUME TWO

"Jealousy is nothing but a mirror, an ugly mirror."

Dr. Bak Nguyen

# 0954

FROM POWERPLAY

"Bitterness kills hope."

Dr. Bak Nguyen

## 0955

FROM 1SELF

"Choice first, values come after."

Dr. Bak Nguyen

## 0956

FROM 1SELF

"Any crisis has the potential to be a RESET BUTTON,
if not total, at least partial."

Dr. Bak Nguyen

## 0957

FROM 1SELF

"Values are boundaries.
Nothing less and nothing more."

Dr. Bak Nguyen

## 0958

FROM 1SELF

"The consensus you need is one with yourself."

Dr. Bak Nguyen

## 0959

FROM 1SELF

"The path is the one in front of you.
It is for you to set it right."

Dr. Bak Nguyen

# 0960
"In the solitude of your cocoon, your only reference points now are your next wins."
**Dr. Bak Nguyen**

# 0961
FROM 1SELF
"The only way to emerge from the cocoon with wings was by focussing on oneself. The only way to grow these wings was to be greater than one."
**Dr. Bak Nguyen**

# 0962
FROM 1SELF
"The dumping of your imperfections will free much energy and resource to feed your journey."
**Dr. Bak Nguyen**

# 0963
FROM 1SELF
"No attachment, no hurt."
**Dr. Bak Nguyen**

## 0964

FROM ALPHA LADDERS VOLUME 2

"Well, if I have one enemy, it is FEAR.
And Fun is my remedy."

Dr. Bak Nguyen

## 0965

FROM THE BOOK OF LEGENDS VOLUME 3

"Grinding has to be from free will to work,
it has to be self-imposed, not imposed!"

Dr. Bak Nguyen

## 0966

FROM THE BOOK OF LEGENDS VOLUME 3

"By now, writing is my way to breathe."

Dr. Bak Nguyen

## 0967

FROM MIRRORS

"To put a feeling into words is the best way to lose
most of its value... but it is still the only way we know."

Dr. Bak Nguyen

## 0968

FROM MIRRORS

"You must survive first in order to thrive one day."

Dr. Bak Nguyen

## 0969
FROM MIRRORS
"Doubt is ignorance fuelled with fear."
**Dr. Bak Nguyen**

## 0970
FROM MIRRORS
"Doubt and pride are
the toxic equation of destruction."
**Dr. Bak Nguyen**

## 0971
FROM MIRRORS
"Your usefulness is your worth."
**Dr. Bak Nguyen**

## 0972
FROM MIRRORS
"The anxiety is real, but the fear can be lifted if the
expectations were to try, not to thrive, at least at first."
**Dr. Bak Nguyen**

## 0973
FROM MIRRORS
"To ignore our failures is to keep them safe
under the shield of pride."
**Dr. Bak Nguyen**

## 0974
FROM MIRRORS
"To fail is everyone's daily story.
The problem is when we pretend otherwise."
Dr. Bak Nguyen

## 0975
FROM MIRRORS
"To put a feeling into words is the best way to lose
most of its value... but it is still the only way we know."
Dr. Bak Nguyen

## 0976
FROM MIRRORS
"Awareness comes, only with the complete
acceptance of oneself."
Dr. Bak Nguyen

## 0977
FROM TO OVERACHIEVER EVERYTHING BEING LAZY
"To be realistic, by definition, is to come back to a
lesser world than those you were dreaming of."
Dr. Bak Nguyen

## 0978

"Get rid of all of the labels that you have been given.
Even those you've created yourself."

Dr. Bak Nguyen

## 0979

"To smell trouble miles away,
look at the people, miles away."

Dr. Bak Nguyen

## 0980

"Once your buffer zone bursts,
you will be running, just to catch up!"

Dr. Bak Nguyen

## 0981

"Our greatest enemy is the ignorance
of how we are built!"

Dr. Bak Nguyen

## 0982

FROM TO OVERACHIEVER EVERYTHING BEING LAZY

"Generate your hormones from your needs
and desires, not your fears."

Dr. Bak Nguyen

## 0983

FROM SHORTCUT VOLUME 1 - HEALING

"Doubt is mainly a side effect
of ignorance falsely disguised."

Dr. Bak Nguyen

## 0984

FROM SHORTCUT VOLUME 1 - HEALING

"Everybody needs healing. Healing and growing
are two faces of the same coin."

Dr. Bak Nguyen

This is **Shortcut volume 1, HEALING**. Welcome to the Alphas.

Dr. BAK NGUYEN

# PART 3

## "THE POWER OF QUOTES"

by Dr. BAK NGUYEN

What is a quote but a recipe of life? If you are just like me, you do not care much about definitions and labels. We care about how they can help us in our everyday life.

As each of the 8 volumes of **SHORTCUT** will comprise of my famous quotes, I will address and developed them with you, with more intent. Sure, you can access the book in which they have been forged to understand the situation and the context. How about a cheat? Yet another hack into the system?

I have 77 famous quotes, famous meaning that they have been the core of my philosophy and the main mindset on which my Momentum and Rise are based from. Well, what I will do within this chapter and the 7 following chapters of the **POWER OF QUOTES** in each of the **SHORTCUT** volumes, is to demonstrate within a few paragraphs, their power and how they have changed my life.

"A quote is no rhetoric. A quote is a formula
to be mastered and leveraged."
Dr. Bak Nguyen

And that is the 2416th quote! Let's not waste time and prove the concept so you too, can master them to leverage your rise with the **POWER OF YOUR BODY**, the **POWER OF YOUR HEART**, and the **POWER OF YOUR MIND**.

The **POWER OF YOUR BODY** is comprised of your needs and hunger. The **POWER OF YOUR HEART** is comprised of your desires The **POWER OF YOUR MIND** is your will. They appear in order of importance, the body first, the heart second and the mind last.

"To be whole is to have access to all of your powers, the body, the heart, and the mind."
Dr. Bak Nguyen

And that is the 2417th quote! Since there are 77 famous quotes, I will explain and share with you shortly their story, 8 at a time, respecting the number of the Dragon. May they inspire you and find their use in the palm of your hands.

**FAMOUS QUOTE 1**

0001
FROM SYMPHONY OF SKILLS
"The pain of the problem has to be greater than the pain of change."
Dr. Bak Nguyen

Change is a pain. Pain is a problem to all. Don't be the problem, even if you have great intentions. Wait for the problem to occurs and then, be the solution. It might be a stupid way to walk in the mud first and then, to clean it after. It is what it is, we are built to not believe in change until it is absolutely necessary.

As a doctor for 20 plus years, that was the key to my success. I needed to help my patients understand their pain first. Only then, I have a chance of making them better. In medicine, that is called consent, informed consent. Skip that step and the resistance will be your greatest enemy.

## FAMOUS QUOTE 2

<br>

### 0004
FROM IDENTITY, ANTHOLOGY OF QUESTS
"Gratitude is the only past with a future."
**Dr. Bak Nguyen**

Just like we can read in the bible and most of the legends and stories, if you turn around and look back, you will be turned into a statue of salt or will find a ghost tracking you. Even if the past is your story, your life happens ahead. That's the flow of life, reverse that and you will pay the consequences.

I am aware of how controversial this quote is, but it is as true as it gets. Now, what about knowledge, education, culture? Those are part of the past too, no?

Well, do not take them as absolute truth, have respect for them, especially, learn and appreciate the process leading to their discovery and you will have mastered the key to evolution.

What is true yesterday can be a half-truth today and a flaw tomorrow. People change, you change, life evolves. Nothing is set in stone, but the respect of the process and of the men and women who walked the path before you.

How do you think that I came to write 100 books? I started with reading most of the books I was drawn to. Then, I sat on them until they made sense.

That took nearly 3 decades, and once in possession of the **KEY OF FORGIVENESS**, I walked my path, honouring my past but with a light and available heart to embrace the future. I can't change the past, only influence the future.

So if I can't change the past, why even care. I simply have to remember where I started from and to whom I owe. The first one serves as a point of reference while the second serves for direction, as a why. And what is the **WHY** but the **POWER OF THE HEART**?

0006

FROM INDUSTRIES' DISRUPTORS

"To walk on thin ice is a dangerous game.
To run is safer. To surf is the easiest."

Dr. Bak Nguyen

This one should sound reversed to many of you. The old saying was to learn to crawl and then to walk before running. I don't believe that flying is even part of the saying. Well, guess what? You have a faulty recipe, one that will keep your feet firmly on the ground!

Go through that saying and see how victim you are from the Gravity. Everything draws you to the soil. Gravity is a law of physic, just like every law of physics, it is relative! Relative, that is your key.

So can you walk on water? Not based on that logic of crawling to walking and eventually running. But walking on water exist, it is called surfing! Have we defied the law of Gravity? No, we compensate it with the law of kinetic.

So life is not solid ground. The ground we are walking on is not even solid, that's an illusion, not to say ignorance! If the ground is moving slowly, it is still moving. Life in the fast lane is moving, only faster.

Walk on water and you will drown, left alone crawling. Embrace that belief and you are stuck to the ground, forget the ocean and the sky. To me, that is not wisdom but ignorance.

Now, understand the law of change and relativity. Embrace the dynamic of change and surf the change. Life is dynamic, would you rather crawl through life, walk through life or surf through life. What I can tell you is that they are all movements, the difference was the amount of friction generated.

And one last thing, how does friction translate in everyday life? As heat and pain. Your choice.

## FAMOUS QUOTE 4

### 0014
FROM CHANGING THE WORLD FROM A DENTAL CHAIR
"Hammering air three times over
and it will become steel."
**Dr. Bak Nguyen**

This is one of my great findings, how to materialize an idea, a vision into reality. Well, a belief, a vision, an idea, however you are calling it, it is just a fragment of air, of your imagination. If you thought of it once, the moment, as powerful as it was, will fade as a moment.

If you relive it more than once, you are making it into an anchor. That anchor can attach you down or serve as a stepping stone, once again, you are the one deciding.

To me, air is air. It takes me the same time to think of smaller air than to dream of space and of the Universe. As it was just air, I allowed myself to dream bigger and bigger. Well, I discovered a great side effect, the bigger the dream, the more the energy.

Some of these great visions leave trails of energy (called vibes) that could last for days and weeks. That was surely a long moment.

Well, that's when I stopped thinking small to embrace dreaming as wildly as it came. Then, I surfed the vibe created. Just like an addict, I grew entitled to that great energy. As it fades away, I have to repeat the process of dreaming the same dream again.

And then, the energy was once more, but as the second time happens, the energy was not as intensive and did not last merely as long. And by the third time, it became merely a small fix.

So I tried something new. I dreamed and surf the vibe. Before the original vibe completely fades, I dream again, the same dream, but with more clarity, pushing forward the imagery and the sensations. I created a second wave riding on the back of the first one. The energy was not adding up but multiplying in intensity and height.

So what do you think that I did? I dreamed a third time on top of the second wave. By the third wave, I created so much energy to ride the ocean.

This is how I grow and build momentum, hammering the same air 3 times over. I do not stop at 3, but the power is undeniable at 3 and the game is getting more and more fun.

If the first wave was just a crazy idea, a dream, the second was a plan and strategy. With the third wave, I have an opportunity and the means to attract people believing in the idea. And with more people, the waves are stacking up, one on top of the next, making the dream into a tornado. Give it a try, and your only regret will be to have waited this long before trying.

Please be mindful of your dream, power is power, you still need to be aware of the consequences.

**FAMOUS QUOTE 5**

0018
FROM THE POWER BEHIND THE ALPHA
"Humility is to know what you are
and recognize what you are not."
Dr. Bak Nguyen

118

Rising starts with healing first. Well, what are we healing from? Of the handicaps and false beliefs forced into us by culture, religion, education, and Conformity. They did not look for dialogue to evolve but to a one-way communication to shape and regulate each of us.

It is not wrong, it has allowed the apparition of the average. With the evolution of Society, we came to replace some of these beliefs with better ones to raise the **average of society**. Today, we stand on the shoulders of all who were before us.

That being said, those who were before built upon what was already there and elevate Society a little bit at a time. That is the only way for us to evolve, accepting change a little at a time until the new change sinks in and is accepted as a new basis.

The order of society depends on the stability of our laws and structures, in other words, it depends on the absorption of the new values without threatening the base. To do so, society and Conformity have put everything in their power to reduce the energy available to a more manageable size.

They did so with intimidation, education, and often the misusage of noble value as Humility. To make sure that their message was getting through without or with less resistance, they called docility, humility. When that did not cut, they stole the name of God and call it Faith.

Don't get me wrong. I am a believer and if there is one fear in my heart is the fear to disappoint God. That being said, my humility is not set in docility, but in the recognition of what and who I am (Confidence) and the recognition of what I am not and still have to learn (Humility).

As I am confident, I am available to listen without judging nor preconceived ideas. As I am humble and secure, I do not have to spend much energy to maintain the appearances nor the maintenance of my own prison.

Knowing what I am not, I now have the freedom to decide to be better or not. What Conformity called arrogance was in fact assurance (the Confidence to ask for questions they do not want to answer or did not have the answer to).

From there, I grew, open and curious to learn and master more and more. Today, I like to think that I have joined our forefathers and foremothers contributing to the evolution of our kind, of our mind.

**FAMOUS QUOTE 6**

0021

FROM MOMENTUM TRANSFER

"To stabilize a momentum, speed up!"

Dr. Bak Nguyen

We addressed earlier the law of physics and its relativity. Well, just like gravity, momentum is a force that needs mastering to be leveraged. If to leverage Gravity, we need the power of kinetic to balance and to surf, will the power of stacking kinetic is called momentum.

A momentum is air stacking up. The air was light at the beginning, but once staked up, it gained in weight exponentially. Weight and power are two faces of the same coin. So if we started light and innocent, very quickly, the momentum that we've created will bear weight and consequences. A new set of laws of Gravity will emerge.

Just like the first time, as we were crawling on solid ground, to beat the new law of Gravity, we must push even harder, faster, before the weight has the time to set. And that's the secret, to move faster than consequences it bears. The **Energy Formula** book will prove that concept in more precise words.


**FAMOUS QUOTE 7**


0034

FROM THE RISE OF THE UNICORN

"To make the world a better place."

**Dr. Bak Nguyen**

If I told you that **HEALING** was the beginning of our journey, finding **WORTH** is the key to finding powers, more and more powers. Only after dropping denial, the healing process could begin. Once healed, I became whole again and was now secure (Confident) and available to find my powers and worth.

Well, powers I did not find looking at what I have been taught, but as I kept my place in society, serving others. Before y reunification, I had a profession and a role in society, treating teeth. I did that successfully with the science I've been trusted with.

Then, as I became more and more aware (whole), I shifted from treating teeth to treating people. Slowly but surely, a little each day, day after day.

I applied all of myself to easing people's pain (dentistry). Keeping my position as a healer, I grew slowly into empowering them to rise and to embrace their desires, becoming a cosmetic dental surgeon.

What I did with their teeth, I now did to their smile. Very quickly, I notice that it did not stop at a smile but had everything to do with their confidence and how they see themselves.

I kept observing. What changed in them got them to act differently and the world started to react differently to them.

And this is how I witness the **power of change** as most of my patients bloom with confidence and beauty.

And I learnt and noticed, I doubled down on. From healing one person at a time, I found better ways to leverage my time and energy to now leave my discovery and formulas for all of you to find, all of you and all of our children, grandchildren, and theirs grandchildren.

I found my powers and worth making the world a better place! And yes, I am sure about the BETTER part since I am healing and empower the blooming of your potential. That's happiness in its purest state.

## FAMOUS QUOTE 8

0045
FROM THE POWER OF YES, VOLUME 1
"Writing books allowed me to evolve
at the speed of my thoughts."
### Dr. Bak Nguyen

That was my way to speed up my healing process. From a book to another, each title was a stepping stone allowing the next one to be built upon. And since I did not wait for permission, I have nothing to wait for. After the completion of a book, I started the next one as the feelings came.

You know what happened? What I felt was the momentum and victory of completing one book but also the need to address the angles I left out of that narrative to keep the logic and progression of the present book. Sometimes it was the logic, some other things it was the public to whom the book was intended to.

I respected the boundaries of a book but once the book completed, I was free to tackle what I left aside. That was also to address what I learnt while writing.

I did not wait and kept dialoguing, with my audience, with you, with my co and guest-authors, with myself. This is how I pushed my evolution at the speed of my thoughts.

I did that and leverage all of the tools available from the democratization of information and the means of production to not only write my books but to edit and publish them, so they are available to all of you.

Editing and publishing, I learnt even more than I bargained for!

This is **Shortcut volume 1, HEALING**. Welcome to the Alphas.

Dr. BAK NGUYEN

# PART 4
## "FAMOUS QUOTES"
by Dr. BAK NGUYEN

## 0001

FROM SYMPHONY OF SKILLS

"The pain of the problem has to be greater than the pain of change."

Dr. Bak Nguyen

## 0002

FROM SYMPHONY OF SKILLS

"Sharing is the way to grow."

Dr. Bak Nguyen

## 0003

FROM LEADERSHIP, PANDORA'S BOX

"One's legend can only begin the day one's Quest of Identity is over."

Dr. Bak Nguyen

## 0004

FROM IDENTITY, ANTHOLOGY OF QUESTS

"Gratitude is the only past with a future."

Dr. Bak Nguyen

## 0005

FROM PROFESSION HEALTH

"Mine was, forgive yourself."

Dr. Bak Nguyen

## 0006
"To walk on thin ice is a dangerous game.
To run is safer. To surf is the easiest."
### Dr. Bak Nguyen

## 0007
"If I have changed the world from a dental chair,
you are all in a better position than I am
to change the world."
### Dr. Bak Nguyen

## 0008
"The day you are fighting to raise the average instead
of beating it, that day, you've joined the leadership."
### Dr. Bak Nguyen

## 0009
"At the end of the day, business is communication."
### Dr. Bak Nguyen

## 0010
FROM INDUSTRIES' DISRUPTORS
"Make leverage of each of your liabilities,
and you will always be moving forward."
**Dr. Bak Nguyen**

## 0011
FROM INDUSTRIES' DISRUPTORS
"I believe in myself and I do it for God,
not the other way around."
**Dr. Bak Nguyen**

## 0012
FROM INDUSTRIES' DISRUPTORS
"Always choose the path of least resistance."
**Dr. Bak Nguyen**

## 0013
FROM INDUSTRIES' DISRUPTORS
"Be mindful of the consequences."
**Dr. Bak Nguyen**

## 0014
FROM CHANGING THE WORLD FROM A DENTAL CHAIR
"Hammering air three times over
and it will become steel."
**Dr. Bak Nguyen**

## 0015

"Mdex, for joy for life."

**Dr. Bak Nguyen**

## 0016

"Confidence is sexy."

**Dr. Bak Nguyen**

## 0017

"Make it happen!"

**Dr. Bak Nguyen**

## 0018

FROM THE POWER BEHIND THE ALPHA

"Humility is to know what you are and to recognize what you are not."

**Dr. Bak Nguyen**

## 0019

FROM MOMENTUM TRANSFER

"On thin ice, speed up, that's how you will eventually learn to fly! "

**Dr. Bak Nguyen**

## 0020

FROM MOMENTUM TRANSFER

"Control with wisdom is called influence."

Dr. Bak Nguyen

## 0021

FROM MOMENTUM TRANSFER

"To stabilize a momentum, speed up!"

Dr. Bak Nguyen

## 0022

FROM HYBRID

"Chords and patterns are the themes of the Universe."

Dr. Bak Nguyen

## 0023

FROM HYBRID

"A weakness is a strength out of reach."

Dr. Bak Nguyen

## 0024

FROM HYBRID

"Look for your next immediate win."

Dr. Bak Nguyen

## 0025

FROM REBOOT, TO GROW FROM MIDLIFE CRISIS

"Don't stop the flow of a river unless you are ready to clean up the flood."

Dr. Bak Nguyen


## 0026

FROM LEVERAGE COMMUNICATION INTO SUCCESS

"Find your worth in the service of others."

Dr. Bak Nguyen


## 0027

FROM LEVERAGE COMMUNICATION INTO SUCCESS

"Humility is not the denial of oneself but the acceptance of one true nature."

Dr. Bak Nguyen


## 0028

FROM THE BOOK OF LEGENDS, VOLUME 1

"We are all born little, as a chicken heart. If we keep an open mind, we will grow into a lion heart. Some will choose to be close-minded and will remain small."

Dr. Bak Nguyen

## 0029

FROM THE BOOK OF LEGENDS, VOLUME 1

"To have an open mind is step one.
To keep growing, one needs an open heart."

Dr. Bak Nguyen

## 0030

FROM THE BOOK OF LEGENDS, VOLUME 1

"Humility is the ability to recognize and to respect
what we are, and stop pretending
to be what we are not."

Dr. Bak Nguyen

## 0031

FROM SELFMADE

"Good things start to happen when you say yes!"

Dr. Bak Nguyen

## 0032

FROM SELFMADE

"Knowledge is the ground of the past.
Hope and Dreams are the air of the future."

Dr. Bak Nguyen

## 0033

FROM SELFMADE

"My deepest fear is to show up before God
and not have enough to show for."

Dr. Bak Nguyen

## 0034

FROM THE RISE OF THE UNICORN

"To make the world a better place."

**Dr. Bak Nguyen**

## 0035

FROM THE RISE OF THE UNICORN

"A Momentum is when it is easier
to keep moving than to stop."

**Dr. Bak Nguyen**

## 0036

FROM CHAMPION MINDSET

"I was open, and I bet on myself."

**Dr. Bak Nguyen**

## 0037

FROM HOW TO WRITE A BOOK IN 30 DAYS

"To keep Momentum, aim for the next win,
as little as it might be."

**Dr. Bak Nguyen**

## 0038

FROM HOW TO WRITE A BOOK IN 30 DAYS

"A quote is a truth from another life,
from a past legacy."

**Dr. Bak Nguyen**

# 0039
FROM HOW TO WRITE A BOOK IN 30 DAYS
"The fewer the words, the better."

Dr. Bak Nguyen

# 0040
FROM POWER, EMOTIONAL INTELLIGENCE
"Align your emotions and your ambitions
to be whole, to be unstoppable."

Dr. Bak Nguyen

# 0041
FROM POWER, EMOTIONAL INTELLIGENCE
"I believe in myself, and I do it for God,
not the other way around."

Dr. Bak Nguyen

# 0042
FROM BRANDING
"I kept the "Dr." on to remind me to always put your
interests before mine."

Dr. Bak Nguyen

# 0043
FROM BRANDING
"Arrogance is not the bragging of our knowledge,
but rather the denial of our ignorance."

Dr. Bak Nguyen

# 0044
FROM HORIZON VOLUME ONE
"I treat people, not teeth."

Dr. Bak Nguyen

# 0045
FROM THE POWER OF YES, VOLUME 1
"Writing books allowed me to evolve
at the speed of my thoughts."

Dr. Bak Nguyen

# 0046
FROM THE POWER OF YES, VOLUME 1
"Speed is my power. Momentum, my expression."

Dr. Bak Nguyen

# 0047
FROM THE POWER OF YES VOLUME 3
"We do not need to choose, only to prioritize."

Dr. Bak Nguyen

# 0048
FROM HOW TO NOT FAIL AS A DENTIST
"Changing the world from a dental chair."

Dr. Bak Nguyen

# 0049
FROM HOW TO NOT FAIL AS A DENTIST

"I am not giving up, I am simply wising up!"

**Dr. Bak Nguyen**

# 0050
FROM HOW TO NOT FAIL AS A DENTIST

"With your money, do not trust anyone but yourself."

**Dr. Bak Nguyen**

# 0051
FROM HUMILITY FOR SUCCESS

"Reading will be cool again!"

**Dr. Bak Nguyen**

# 0052
FROM HUMILITY FOR SUCCESS

"Until it is done, it is air, good air but only air."

**Dr. Bak Nguyen**

# 0053
FROM MASTERMIND

"You can cheat, legally, by learning
about shortcuts and leveraging."

**Dr. Bak Nguyen**

## 0054

FROM PLAYBOOK INTRODUCTION VOLUME 1

"Nothing will last forever, and nothing is free."

Dr. Bak Nguyen

## 0055

FROM PLAYBOOK INTRODUCTION VOLUME 2

"Be careful since doubts is a pet
that you are feeding."

Dr. Bak Nguyen

## 0056

FROM PLAYBOOK INTRODUCTION VOLUME 2

"Reach for your next win as soon as possible,
and build on it!"

Dr. Bak Nguyen

## 0057

FROM AMONGST THE ALPHAS, VOLUME 2

"Be bold, confident, and humble."

Dr. Bak Nguyen

## 0058

FROM AMONGST THE ALPHAS, VOLUME 2

"Growth happens at the giving end,
not the receiving one."

Dr. Bak Nguyen

# 0059

FROM SUCCESS IS A CHOICE

"Be bold, be flexible, act fast and stay humble."

**Dr. Bak Nguyen**

# 0060

FROM SUCCESS IS A CHOICE

"To succeed, be flexible."

**Dr. Bak Nguyen**

# 0061

FROM 90 DAYS CHALLENGE

"In times of crisis, one has to reinvent oneself."

**Dr. Bak Nguyen**

# 0062

FROM RISING

"To matter, serve."

**Dr. Bak Nguyen**

# 0063

FROM RISING

"There is no free money."

**Dr. Bak Nguyen**

# 0064

FROM AFTERMATH

"For the first time of our lifetime,
all the interests of the world are aligned."

**Dr. Bak Nguyen**

## 0065

FROM AFTERMATH

"In times of crisis, it is the perfect opportunity
to reinvent who we are. "

**Dr. Bak Nguyen**

## 0066

FROM AFTERMATH

"Yes, we can have it all!"

**Dr. Bak Nguyen**

## 0067

FROM TORNADO

"History will say that to celebrate one world record,
we scored two more!"

**Dr. Bak Nguyen**

## 0068

FROM TORNADO

"The only way to keep overdelivering
is playing, all-in!"

**Dr. Bak Nguyen**

## 0069

FROM TORNADO

"Dream and the means will come."

**Dr. Bak Nguyen**

# 0070
FROM ALPHA LADDERS VOLUME ONE

"All good things start with a YES."

Dr. Bak Nguyen

# 0071
FROM ALPHA LADDERS VOLUME 2

"Growth occurs at the giving end, always."

Dr. Bak Nguyen

# 0072
FROM THE CONFESSION OF AN OVERACHIEVER

"Being lazy doesn't mean that you don't have to do shit, it means that you don't have to go through shit to get things done."

Dr. Bak Nguyen

# 0073
FROM TO OVERACHIEVER EVERYTHING BEING LAZY

"Arrogance is not the recognition of who we are but the denial of what we are not."

Dr. Bak Nguyen

## 0074
FROM TO OVERACHIEVER EVERYTHING BEING LAZY

"You call me doctor to remind me to always put your needs before mine."

Dr. Bak Nguyen

## 0075
FROM TO OVERACHIEVER EVERYTHING BEING LAZY

"Nowadays, influence is power without liability."

Dr. Bak Nguyen

## 0076
FROM TO OVERACHIEVER EVERYTHING BEING LAZY

"I told you that everything in life is a trade. Be careful of what you are trading."

Dr. Bak Nguyen

## 0077
FROM SHORTCUT VOLUME 1 - HEALING

"Fear is a disease and it must be treated like one."

Dr. Bak Nguyen

This is **Shortcut volume 1, HEALING**. Welcome to the Alphas.

Dr. BAK NGUYEN

# CONCLUSION

by Dr. BAK NGUYEN

And with this ends our first journey from **SHORTCUT**, the healing. If it all starts with **HEALING**, I hope that you were inspired by my journey. You too, have dropped your denials and have freed that much-needed energy and attention to start your healing process.

Forget perfection, expectations, judgments, and labelling. We each have our own timing and pace. If the first step to healing was to Dr.op denial, the second one is to accept who we are, our limits, and powers.

"Timing and pace are part of who and what we are."
Dr. Bak Nguyen

That's quote number 2418! What is a quote but the expression of a reality and an affirmation? As we all need to heal from what was done to us, even with the best of intention, we all grow, looking for happiness. And yet, we were all born happy in the first place.

In other words, we are spending most of our adult and useful life to find back our true nature and destiny. And this is what it means **to be**. Ever wonder why **to have** does not always leads you to happiness? Well, you just have your answer.

As nothing in life is free, there is always a trade: we are trading being for having. That is okay to feed our needs and hunger. Then we kept the same recipe to feed our desires. That still passes. The cancer and gangrene of the soul happen as we applied the same recipe to feed our mind and will.

The key to hunger was to grow and to become stronger to feed. The key to desire was to grow and to become even bigger to provide. How about the key to will power? Well, if we are that stronger and that bigger learning to feed and to provide, we do not need to take our determination from our will as much, we only need to sort our mindsets and all that we have accumulated so far.

We know, we do not have knowledge. In other words, we know and we keep moving forward, secure and available, ready to embrace the next opportunity, the next challenge is to grow and learn from that one too. Our knowledge does not define who we are, those are just tools.

And **WILL POWER**? Well, that is power, simply the lesser of the main powers available to us, the **POWER OF THE BODY**, the **POWER OF THE HEART**, and the **POWER OF THE MIND**.

No matter the powers you master and leverage, to yield powers, you must be secure and available first, in other words, you must be whole. This is why **HEALING** is the first step of your journey, of my journey, of each of our legends.

"One's legend can only begin the day
one's Quest of Identity is over."
Dr. Bak Nguyen

You don't have to be ambitious nor to want to change the world, you still need to heal to find happiness, your happiness. This one is universal.

If we spent 331 quotes healing, I spent the next 77 quotes showing you what is coming next, of how to leverage the powers once you are whole.

What to do with your powers is for you and you alone to decide. I urge you to always consider the consequences and the collaterals before exercising your powers and momentum.

The hope of this book is that you have within your the power and energy to heal and to be whole. In other words, you hold within you the key to your happiness and freedom.

This is just the first step on the journey to your power. **SHORTCUT** is comprised of 8 volumes, each of them, containing the secrets and power to the next stage. After **HEALING**, **GROWTH** is the next volume. **LEADERSHIP**, **CONFIDENCE**, **SUCCESS**, **POWER**, **HAPPINESS**, and **DOCTORS** (Healers) are the next stages ahead.

Congratulation, you have begun your walk to **REUNIFICATION**, your **Quest of Identity**. The next stages will ease your way ahead and help your transition from looking for your name, to walk your legend.

This is **Shortcut volume 1, HEALING**. Welcome to the Alphas.

It all started with healing.
Heal to find your freedom.
Heal to find your powers.
Heal to be happy and whole.

**Dr. BAK NGUYEN**

# ANNEX

GLOSSARY OF Dr. BAK's LIBRARY

# 1

## 1SELF -080

### REINVENT YOURSELF FROM ANY CRISIS
BY Dr. BAK NGUYEN

In 1SELF is about to reinvent yourself to rise from any crisis. Written in the midst of the COVID war, now more than ever, we need hope and the know-how to bridge the future. More than just the journey of Dr. Bak, this time, Dr. Bak is sharing his journey with mentors and people who built part of the world as we know it. Interviewed in this book, CHRISTIAN TRUDEAU, former CEO and FOUNDER of BCE EMERGIS (BELL CANADA), he also digitalized the Montreal Stock Exchange.RON KLEIN, American Innovator, inventor of the magnetic stripe of the credit card, of MLS (Multi-listing services) and the man who digitalized WALL STREET bonds markets.ANDRE CHATELAIN, former first vice-president of the MOVEMENT DESJARDINS. Dr. JEAN DE SERRES, former CEO of HEMA QUEBEC. These men created billions in values and have changed our lives, even without us knowing. They all come together to share their experiences and knowledge to empower each and everyone to emerge stronger from this crisis, from any crisis.

# A

## AFTERMATH -063
### BUSINESS AFTER THE GREAT PAUSE
BY Dr. BAK NGUYEN & Dr. ERIC LACOSTE

In AFTERMATH, Dr. Bak joins forces with Community leader and philanthrope Dr. Eric Lacoste. Two powerful minds and forces of nature in the reaction to the worst economic meltdown in modern times. We are all victims of the CORONA virus. Both just like humans have learned to adapt to survive, so is our economy. Most business structures and management philosophies are inherited from the age of industrialization and beyond. COVID-19 has shut down the world economy with months. At the time of the AFTERMATH, the truth is many corporations and organizations will either have to upgrade to the INFORMATION AGE or disappear. More than the INFORMATION upgrade, the era of SOCIAL MEDIA and the MILLENNIALS are driving a revolution in the core philosophy of all organizations. Profit is not king anymore, support is. In this time and age where a teenager with a social account can compete with the million dollars PR firm, social implication is now the new cornerstone. Those who will adapt will prevail and prosper, while the resistance and old guards will soon be forgotten as fossils of a past era.

## ALPHA LADDERS -075
### CAPTAIN OF YOUR DESTINY
BY Dr. BAK NGUYEN & JONAS DIOP

In ALPHA LADDERS, Dr. Bak is sharing his private conversation and board meetings with 2 of his trusted lieutenants, strategist Jonas Diop and international Counsellor, Brenda Garcia. As both the Dr. Bak and ALPHA brands are gaining in popularity and traction, it was time to get the movement to the next level. Now, it's about building a community and to help everyone willing to become ALPHAS to find their powers. Dr. Bak is a natural recruiter of ALPHAS and peers. He also spent the last 20 years plus, training and mentoring proteges. Now comes the time to empower more and more proteges to become ALPHAS. ALPHAS LADDERS is the journey of how Dr. Bak went from a product of Conformity to rise into a force of Nature, know as a kind tornado. In ALPHA LADDERS Jonas pushed Dr. Bak to retrace each of the steps of his awakening, steps that we can breakdown and reproduce for ourselves. The goal is to empower each willing individual to become the ultimate Captain of his or her destiny, and to do it, again and again. Welcome to the Alphas.

## ALPHA LADDERS 2 -081
### SHAPING LEADERS AND ACHIEVERS
BY Dr. BAK NGUYEN & BRENDA GARCIA

In ALPHA LADDERS 2, Dr. Bak is sharing the second part of his private conversation and board meetings with his trusted lieutenants. This time it is with international Counsellor, Brenda Garcia that the dialogue is taking place. In this second tome, the journey is taken to the next level. If the first tome was about the WHYs and the HOWs at an individual level, this tome is about the WHYs and the HOWs at the societal level. Through the lens of her background in international relations and diplomacy, Brenda now has the mission to help Dr. Bak establish structures, not only for his emerging organization and legacy, THE ALPHAS, but to also inspire all the other leaders and structures of our society. To do this, Brenda is taking Dr. Bak on an anthropological, sociological and philosophical journey to revisit different historical key moments in various fields and eras, going as far back as in ancient Greece at the dawn of democracy, all the way to the golden era of modern multilateralism embodied by the UN structure. Learning from the legacies of prominent figures going from Plato to Ban Ki Moon, Martin Luther King or Nelson Mandela, to Machiavelli, Marx and Simone de Beauvoir, Brenda and Dr. Bak are attempting to grasp the essence of structure and hierarchy, their goal being to empower each willing individual to become the ultimate Captain of their own success, to climb up the ladders no matter how high it is, and to build their legacy one step at a time.

## AMONGST THE ALPHAS -058
BY Dr. BAK NGUYEN, with Dr. MARIA KUNDSTATER, Dr. PAUL OUELLETTE and Dr. JEREMY KRELL

In AMONGST THE ALPHAS Dr. Bak opens the blueprint of the next level with the hope that everyone can be better, bigger, wiser, but above all, a philosophy of Life that if, well applied, can bring inspiration to life. The Alphas rose in the midst of the COVID war as an International Collaboration to empower individuals to rise from the global crisis. Joining Dr. Bak are some of the world thinkers and achievers, the Alphas. Doctors, business people, thinkers, achievers, influencers, they are coming together to define what is an Alpha and his or her role, making the world a better place. This isn't the American dream, it is the human dream, one that can help you make History. Joining Dr. Bak are 3 Alpha authors, Dr. Maria Kundstater, Dr. Paul Ouellette and Dr. Jeremy Krell. This book started with questions from coach Jonas Diop. Welcome to the Alphas.

## AMONGST THE ALPHAS vol.2 -059
### ON THE OTHER SIDE
BY Dr. BAK NGUYEN with Dr. JULIO REYNAFARJE, Dr. LINA DUSEVICIUTE and Dr. DUC-MINH LAM-DO

In AMONGST THE ALPHAS 2. Dr. Bak continues to explore the meaning of what it is to be an Alpha and how to act amongst Alphas, because as the saying taught us: alone one goes fast, together we goes far. Some people see the problem. Some people look at the problem, some people created the problem. Some people leverage the problem into solutions and opportunities. Well, all of those people are Alphas. Networking and leveraging one another, their powers and reach are beyond measure. And one will keep the other in line too. Joining Dr. Bak are 3 Alphas from around the world coming together to share and collaborate, Dr. DUSEVICIUTE, Dr. LAM-DO and Dr. REYNAFARJE. This isn't the American dream, it is the human dream, one that can help you make History. Welcome to the Alphas.

# B

## BOOTCAMP -071
### BOOKS TO REWRITE MINDSETS INTO WINNING STATES OF MIND
BY Dr. BAK NGUYEN

In BOOTCAMP 8 BOOKS TO REWRITE MINDSETS INTO WINNING STATES OF MIND, Dr. Bak is taking you into his past, before the visionary entrepreneur, before the world records, before the Industry's disruptor status. Here are 8 of the books that changed Dr. Bak's thinking and, therefore, reset his evolution into the course we now know him for. BOOTCAMP: 8 BOOKS TO REWRITE MINDSETS INTO WINNING STATES OF MIND, is a Bootcamp of 8 weeks for anyone looking to experience Dr. Bak's training to become THE Dr. BAK you came to know and love. This book will summarize how each title changed Dr. Bak mindset into a state of mind and how he applied that to rewrite his destiny. 8 books to read, that's 8 weeks of Bootcamp to access the power of your MIND and of your WILL. Are you ready for a change?

## BRANDING -044
## BALANCING STRATEGY AND EMOTIONS
BY Dr. BAK NGUYEN

BRANDING is communication to its most powerful state. Branding is not just about communicating anymore but about making a promise, about establishing a relation, about generating an emotion. More than once, Dr. Bak proved himself to be a master, communicating and branding his ideas into flags attracting interest and influences, nationally and internationally. In BRANDING, Dr. Bak shares a very unique and personal journey, branding Dr. Bak. How does he go from Dr. Nguyen, a loved and respected dentist to becoming Dr. Bak, a world anchor hosting THE ALPHAS in the medical and financial world?More than a personal journey, BRANDING helps to break down the steps to elevate someone with nothing else but the force of his or her spirit. Welcome to the Alphas.

# C

## CHANGING THE WORLD FROM A DENTAL CHAIR -007
BY Dr. BAK NGUYEN

Since he has received the EY's nomination for entrepreneur of the year for his startup Mdex & Co, Dr. Bak Nguyen has pushed the opportunity to the next level. Speaker, author, and businessman, Dr. Bak is a true entrepreneur and industries' disruptor. To compensate for the startup's status of Mdex & Co, he challenged himself to write a book based on the EY's questionnaire to share an in-depth vision of his company. With "Changing the World from a dental chair" Dr. Bak is sharing his thought process and philosophy to his approach to the industry. Not looking to revolutionize but rather to empower, he became, despite himself, an industries disruptor: an entrepreneur who has established a new benchmark. Dr. Bak Nguyen is a cosmetic dentist and visionary businessman who won the GRAND HOMAGE prize of "LYS de la Diversité" 2016, for his contribution as a citizen and entrepreneur in the community. He also holds recognitions from the Canadian Parliament and the Canadian Senate.

In 2003, he founded Mdex, a dental company upon which in 2018, he launched the most ambitious private endeavour to reform the dental industry, Canada wide. He wrote seven books covering ENTREPRENEURSHIP, LEADERSHIP, QUEST of IDENTITY, and now, PROFESSION HEALTH. Philosopher, he has close to his heart the quest of happiness of the people surrounding him, patients, and colleagues alike. Those projects have allowed Dr. Nguyen to attract interests from the international and diplomatic community and he is now the centre of a global discussion on the wellbeing and the future of the health profession. It is in that matter that he shares with you his thoughts and encourages the health community to share their own stories.

## CHAMPION MINDSET -039
## LEARNING TO WIN
BY Dr. BAK NGUYEN & CHRISTOPHE MULUMBA

CHAMPION MINDSET is the encounter of the business world and the professional sports world. Industries' Disruptor Dr. BAK NGUYEN shares his wisdom and views with the HAMMER, CFL Football Star, Edmonton's Eskimos CHRISTOPHE MULUMBA on how to leverage on the champion mindset to create successful entrepreneurs. Writing and challenging each other, they discovered the parallels and the difference of both worlds, but mainly, the recipe for leveraging from one to succeed in the other, from champions and entrepreneurs to WINNERS. Build and score your millions, it is a matter of mindset! This is CHAMPION MINDSET.

# E

## EMPOWERMENT -069
BY Dr. BAK NGUYEN

In EMPOWERMENT, Dr. Bak's 69th book, writing a book every 8 days for 8 weeks in a row to write the next world record of writing 72 books/36 months, Dr. Bak is taking a rest, sharing his inner feelings, inspiration, and motivation. Much more than his dairy, EMPOWERMENT is the key to walk in his footsteps and to comprehend the process of an overachiever. Dr. Bak's helped and inspired countless people to find their voice, to live their dream, and to be the better version of themselves. Why is he sharing as much and keep sharing? Why is he going that fast, always further and further, why and how is he keeping his inspiration and momentum? Those are all the answers EMPOWERMENT will deliver to you. This book might be one of the fastest Dr. Bak has written, not because of time constraints but from inspiration, pure inspiration to share and to grow. There is always a dark side to each power, two faces to a coin. Well, this is the less prominent facets of Dr. Bak Momentum and success, the road to his MINDSET.

# F

## FORCES OF NATURE -015
### FORGING THE CHARACTER OF WINNERS
BY Dr. BAK NGUYEN

In FORCES OF NATURE, Dr. Bak is giving his all. This is his 15 books written within 15 months. It is the end of a marathon to set the next world record. For the occasion, he wanted to end with a big bang! How about a book with all of his biggest challenges? A Quest of Identity, a journey looking for his name and powers, Dr. Bak is borrowing with myths and legends to make this journey universal. Yes, this is Dr. Bak's mythology. Demons, heroes and Gods, there are forces of Nature that we all meet on our way for our name. Some will scare us, some will fight us, some will manipulate us. We can flee, we can hide, we can fight. What we do will define our next encounter and the one after. A tale of personal growth, a journey to find power and purpose, Dr. Bak is showing us the path to freedom, the Path of Life. Welcome to the Alphas.

# H

## HORIZON, BUILDING UP THE VISION -045
### VOLUME ONE
BY Dr. BAK NGUYEN

Dr. Bak is opening up at your demand! Many of you are following Dr. Bak online and are asking to know more about his lifestyle. This is how he has chosen to respond: sharing his lifestyle as he traveled the world and what he learned in each city to come to build his Mindset as a driver and a winner. Here are 10 destinations (over 69 that will be following in the next volumes...) in which he shares his journey. New York, Quebec, Paris, Punta Cana, Monaco, Los Angeles, Nice, Holguin, the journey happened over twenty years.

## HORIZON, ON THE FOOTSTEP OF TITANS -048
## VOLUME TWO
BY Dr. BAK NGUYEN

Dr. Bak is opening up at your demand! Many of you are following Dr. Bak online and are asking to know more about his lifestyle. This is how he has chosen to respond: sharing his lifestyle as he traveled the world and what he learned in each city to come to build his Mindset as a driver and a winner. Here are 9 destinations (over 72 that will be following in the next volumes...) in which he shares his journey. Hong Kong, London, Rome, San Francisco, Anaheim, and more..., the journey happened over twenty years. Dr. Bak is sharing with you his feelings, impressions, and how they shaped his state of mind and character into Dr. Bak. From a dreamer to a driver and a builder, the journey started since he was 3. Wealth is a state of mind, and a state of mind is the basis of the drive. Find out about the mind of an Industry's disruptor.

## HORIZON, Dr.EAMING OF THE FUTURE -068
## VOLUME THREE
BY Dr. BAK NGUYEN

Dr. Bak is back. From the midst of confinement, he remembers and writes about what life was, when traveling was a natural part of Life. It will come back. Now more than ever, we need to open both our hearts and minds to fight fear and intolerance. Writing from a time of crisis, he is sharing the magic and psychological effect of seeing the world and how it has shaped his mindset. Here are 9 other destinations (over 75) in which he shares his journey. Beijing, Key West, Madrid, Amsterdam, Marrakech and more..., the journey happened over twenty years.

## HOW TO NOT FAIL AS A DENTIST -047
BY Dr. BAK NGUYEN

In HOW TO NOT FAIL AS A DENTIST, Dr. Bak is given 20 plus years of experience and knowledge of what it is to be a dentist on the ground. PROFESSIONAL INTELLIGENCE, FINANCIAL INTELLIGENCE and MANAGEMENT INTELLIGENCE are the fields that any dentist will have to master for a chance to success and a shot for happiness practicing dentistry. Where ever you are starting your career as a new graduate or a veteran in the field looking to reach the next level, this is book smart and street smart all into one. This is Million Dollar Mindset applied to dentistry. We won't be making a millionaire out of you from this book, we will be giving you a shot to happiness and success. The million will follow soon enough.

## HOW TO WRITE A BOOK IN 30 DAYS -042
BY Dr. BAK NGUYEN

In HOW TO WRITE YOUR BOOK IN 30 DAYS, Dr. Bak has crafted writing skills and techniques that can be shared and mastered. This book is mainly about structure and how to keep moving forward, avoiding the hit of the INSPIRATION WALL. You will find a wealth of wisdom from his experience writing your first, second, or even 10th book. Dr. Bak is sharing his secrets writing books, having written himself 72 books within 36 months. Visionary businessman, doctor in dentistry, Dr. Bak describes himself as a Dentist by circumstances, a communicator by passion, and an entrepreneur by nature.

## HOW TO WRITE A SUCCESSFUL BUSINESS PLAN -049
BY Dr. BAK NGUYEN & ROUBA SAKR

In HOW TO WRITE A SUCCESSFUL BUSINESS PLAN, Dr. Bak is given 20 plus years of experience and knowledge of what it is to be an entrepreneur and more importantly, how to have the investors and banks on your side. Being an entrepreneur is surely not something you learn from school, but there are steps to master so you can communicate your views and vision. That's the only way you will have financing.Writing a business is only not a mandatory stop only for the bankers, but an essential step to every entrepreneur, to know the direction and what's coming next. A business plan is also not set in stone, if there is a truth in business is that nothing will go as planned. Writing down your business plan the first time will prepare you to adapt and to overcome the challenges and surprises. For most entrepreneurs, a business is a passion. To most investors and all banks, a business is a system. Your business plan is the map to that system. However unique your ideas and business are, the mapping follows the same steps and pattern.

## HUMILITY FOR SUCCESS -051
### BALANCING STRATEGY AND EMOTIONS
BY Dr. BAK NGUYEN

HUMILITY FOR SUCCESS is exploring the emotional discomforts and challenges champions, and overachievers put themselves through. Success is never done overnight and on the way, just like the pain and the struggles aren't enough, we are dealing with the doubts, the haters, and those who like to tell us how to live our lives and what to do. At the same time, nothing of worth can be achieved alone. Every legend has a cast of characters, allies, mentors, companions, rivals, and foes. So one needs the key to social behaviour. HUMILITY FOR SUCCESS is exploring the matter and will help you sort out beliefs from values, peers from friends. Humility is much more about how we see ourselves than how others see us. For any entrepreneur and champion, our daily is to set our mindset right, and to perfect our skills, not to fit in. There is a world where CONFIDENCE grows is in synergy with HUMILITY. As you set the right label on the right belief, you will be able to grow and to leave the lies and haters far behinds. This is HUMILITY FOR SUCCESS.

## HYBRID -011
### THE MODERN QUEST OF IDENTITY
BY Dr. BAK NGUYEN

## IDENTITY -004
## THE ANTHOLOGY OF QUESTS
BY Dr. BAK NGUYEN

What if John Lennon was still alive and running for president today? What kind of campaign will he be running? IDENTIFY -THE ANTHOLOGY OF QUESTS is about the quest each of us has to undertake, sooner or later, THE QUEST OF IDENTITY. Citizen of the world, aim to be one, the one, one whole, one unity, made of many. That's the anthology of life! Start with your one, find your unity, and your legend will start. We are all small-minded people anyway! We need each other to be one! We need each other to be happy, so we, so you, so I, can be happy. This is the chorus of life. This is our song! Citizens of the world, I salute you! This is the first tome of the IDENTITY QUEST. FORCES OF NATURE (tome 2) will be following in SUMMER 2021. Also under development, Tome 3 - THE CONQUEROR WITHIN will start production soon.

## INDUSTRIES DISRUPTORS -006
BY Dr. BAK NGUYEN

INDUSTRIES DISRUPTORS is a strange title, one that sparkles mixed feelings. A disruptor is someone making a difference, and since we, in general, do not like change, the label is mostly negative. But a disruptor is mostly someone who sees the same problem and challenge from another angle. The disruptor will tackle that angle and come up with something new from something existent. That's evolution! In INDUSTRIES DISRUPTORS, Dr. Bak is joining forces with James Stephan-Usypchuk to share with us what is going on in the minds and shoes of those entrepreneurs disrupting the old habits. Dr. Bak is changing the world from a dental chair, disrupting the dental, and now the book industry. James is a maverick in the Intelligence space, from marketing to Artificial Intelligence. Coming from very different backgrounds and industries, they end up telling very similar stories. If disruptors change the world, well, their story proves that disruptors can be made and forged. Here's the recipe. Here are their stories.

# K

**KRYPTO** -040
TO SAVE THE WORLD
BY Dr. BAK NGUYEN & ILYAS BAKOUCH

# L

**LEADERSHIP** -003
PANDORA'S BOX
BY Dr. BAK NGUYEN

LEADERSHIP, PANDORA'S BOX is 21 presidential speeches for a better tomorrow for all of us. It aims to drive HOPE and motivation into each and every one of us. Together we can make the difference, we hold such power. Covering themes from LOYALTY to GENEROSITY, from FREEDOM and INTELLIGENCE to DOUBTS and DEATH, this is not the typical presidential or motivational speeches that we are used to. LEADERSHIP PANDORA'S BOX will surf your emotions first, only to dive with you to touch the core and soul of our meaning: to matter. This is not a Quest of Identity, but the cry to rally as a species, to raise our heads toward the future, and to move forward as a WHOLE. Not a typical Dr. Bak's book, LEADERSHIP, PANDORA'S BOX is a must-read for all of you looking for hope and purpose, all of us, citizens of the world.

**LEVERAGE** -014
COMMUNICATION INTO SUCCESS

BY Dr. BAK NGUYEN

In LEVERAGE COMMUNICATION TO SUCCESS, Dr. Bak shares his secret and mindsets to elevate an idea into a vision and a vision into an endeavour. Some endeavours will be a project, some others will become companies, and some will grow into a movement. It does not matter, each started with great communication.Communication is a very vast concept, education, sale, sharing, empowering, coaching, preaching, entertaining. Those are all different kinds of communication. The intent differs, the audiences vary, the messages are unique but the frame can be templated and mastered. In LEVERAGE COMMUNICATION TO SUCCESS, Dr. Bak is loyal to his core, sharing only what he knows best, what he has done himself. This book is dedicated to communicating successfully in business.

# M

## MASTERMIND, 7 WAYS INTO THE BIG LEAGUE -052
BY Dr. BAK NGUYEN & JONAS DIOP

MASTERMIND, 7 WAYS INTO THE BIG LEAGUE is the result of the encounter of business coach Jonas Diop and Dr. Bak. As a professional podcaster and someone always seeking the truth and ways to leverage success and performance, coach Jonas is putting Dr. Bak to the test, one that should reveal his secret to overachieve month after month, accumulating a new world record every month. Follow those two great minds as they push each other to surpass themselves, each in their own way and own style. MASTERMIND, 7 WAYS INTO THE BIG LEAGUE is more than a roadmap to success, it is a journey and a live testimony as you are turning the pages, one by one.

## MIDAS TOUCH -065
POST-COVID DENTISTRY
BY Dr. BAK NGUYEN, Dr. JULIO REYNAFARJE AND Dr. PAUL OUELLETTE

MIDAS TOUCH, is the memoir of what happened in the ALPHAS SUMMIT in the midst of the GREAT PAUSE as great minds throughout the world in the dental field are coming together. As the time of competition is obsolete, the new era of collaboration is blooming. This is the 3rd book of the ALPHAS, after AFTERMATH and RELEVANCY, all written in the midst of confinement. Dr. Julio Reynafarje is bearing this initiative, to share with you the secret of a successful and lasting relationship with your patients, balancing science and psychology, kindness, and professionalism. He personally invited the ALPHAS to join as co-author, Dr. Paul Ouellette, and Dr. Paul Dominique, and Dr. Bak.Together, they have more than 100 years of combined experience, wisdom, trade, skills, philosophy, and secrets to share with you to empower you in the rebuilding of the dental profession in the aftermath of COVID. RELEVANCY was about coming together and to rebuild the future. MIDAS TOUCH is about how to build, one treatment plan at a time, one story at a time, one smile at a time.

## MINDSET ARMORY -050
BY Dr. BAK NGUYEN

MINDSET ARMORY is Dr. Bak's 49th book, days after he completed his world record of writing 48 books within 24 months, on top of being a CEO of Mdex & Co and a full-time cosmetic dentist. Dr. Bak is undoubtedly an OVERACHIEVER. From his last books, he has shared more and more of his lifestyle and how it forged his winning mindset. Within MINDSET ARMORY, Dr. Bak is sharing with us his tools, how he found them, forged them, and leverage them. Just like any warrior needs a shield, a sword, and a ride, here are Dr. Bak's. For any entrepreneur, the road to success is a long and winding journey. On the way, some will find allies and foes. Some allies will become foes, and some foes might become allies. In today's competitive world, the only constant is change. With the right tool, it is possible to achieve. The right tool, the right mindset. This is MINDSET ARMORY.

## MIRROR -085
BY Dr. BAK NGUYEN

MIRROR is the theme for a personal book. Not only to Dr. Bak but to all of us looking to reach beyond who and what we actually are. MIRROR is special in the fact that it is not only the content of the book that is of worth but the process in which Dr. Bak shared his own evolution. To go beyond who we are, one must grow every day. And how do you compare your growth and how far have you reach? Looking in the mirror. In all of Dr. Bak's writing, looking at the past is a trap to avoid at all costs. Looking in the mirror, is that any better? Share Dr. Bak's way to push and keep pushing himself without friction nor resistance. Please read that again. To evolve without friction or resistance... that is the source of infinite growth and the unification of the Quest for Power and the Quest of Happiness.

## MOMENTUM TRANSFER -009
BY Dr. BAK NGUYEN & Coach DINO MASSON

How to be successful in your business and in your life? Achieve Your Biggest Goals With MOMENTUM TRANSFER. START THE BUSINESS YOU WANT - AND BRING IT NEXT LEVEL! GET THE LIFE YOU ALWAYS WANTED - AND IMPROVE IT! TAKE ANY PROJECTS YOU HAVE - AND MAKE IT THE BEST! In this powerful book, you'll discover what a small business owner learned from a millionaire and successful entrepreneur. He applied his mentor's principles and is explaining them in full detail in this book. The small business owner wrote the book he has always wanted to read and went from the verge of bankruptcy to quadrupling his revenues in less than 9 months and improve his personal life by increasing his energy and bring back peacefulness. Together, the millionaire and the small business owner are sharing their most valuable business and life lessons to the world. The most powerful book to increase your momentum in your business and your life introduces simple and radical life-changing concepts: Multiply your business revenues by finding the Eye of your Momentum - increase your energy by building and feeding your own Momentum - How to increase your confidence with these simple steps - How to transfer your new powerful energy into other aspects of your business and life - How to set goals and achieve them (even crush them!)- How to always tap into an effortless and limitless force within you- And much, much more!

# P

## PLAYBOOK INTRODUCTION -055
BY Dr. BAK NGUYEN

In PLAYBOOK INTRODUCTION, Dr. Bak is open the door to all the newcomers and aspirant entrepreneurs who are looking at where and when to start. Based on questions of two college students wanting to know how to start their entrepreneurial journey, Dr. Bak dives into his experiences to empower the next generation, not about what they should do, but how he, Dr. Bak, would have done it today. This is an important aspect to recognize in the business world, the world has changed since the INFORMATION AGE and the advent of the millenniums into the market. Most matrix and know-how have to be adapted to today's speed and accessibility to the information. We are living at the INFORMATION AGE, this book is the precursor to the ABUNDANCE AGE, at least to those open to embrace the opportunity.

## PLAYBOOK INTRODUCTION 2 -056
BY Dr. BAK NGUYEN

In PLAYBOOK INTRODUCTION 2, Dr. Bak continuing the journey to welcome the newcomers and aspirant entrepreneurs looking at where and when to start. If the first volume covers the mindset, the second is covering much more in-depth the concept of debt and leverage.This is an important aspect to recognize in the business world, the world has changed since the INFORMATION AGE and the advent of the millenniums into the market. Most matrix and know-how have to be adapted to today's speed and accessibility to the information. We are living at the INFORMATION AGE, this book is the precursor to the ABUNDANCE AGE, at least to those open to embrace the opportunity.

## POWER -043
### EMOTIONAL INTELLIGENCE
BY Dr. BAK NGUYEN

IN POWER, EMOTIONAL INTELLIGENCE, Dr. Bak is sharing his experiences and secrets leveraging on his EMOTIONAL INTELLIGENCE, a power we all have within. From SYMPATHY, having others opening up to you, to ACTIVE LISTENING, saving you time and energy; from EMPATHY, allowing you to predict the future to INFLUENCE, enabling you to draft the future, not to forget the power of the crowd with MOMENTUM, you are now in possession of power in tune with nature, yourself. It is a unique take on the subject to empower you to find your powers and your destiny. Visionary businessman, doctor in dentistry, Dr. Bak describes himself as a Dentist by circumstances, a communicator by passion, and an entrepreneur by nature.

## POWERPLAY -078
### HOW TO BUILD THE PERFECT TEAM
BY Dr. BAK NGUYEN

In POWERPLAY, HOW TO BUILD THE PERFECT TEAM, Dr. Bak is sharing with you his experience, perspective, and mistake traveling the journey of the entrepreneur. A serial entrepreneur himself, he started venture only with a single partner as team to build companies with a director of human resources and a board of directors. POWERPLAY is not a story, it is the HOW TO build the perfect team, knowing that perfection is a lie. So how can one build a team that will empower his or her vision? How to recruit, how to train, how to retain? Those are all legitimate questions. And all of those won't matter if the first question isn't answered: what is the reason for the team? There is the old way to hire and the new way to recruit. Yes, Human Resources is all about mindset too! This journey is one of introspection, of leadership, and a cheat sheet to build, not only the perfect team but the team that will empower your legacy to the next level.

## PROFESSION HEALTH - TOME ONE -005
### THE UNCONVENTIONAL QUEST OF HAPPINESS
BY Dr. BAK NGUYEN, Dr. MIRJANA SINDOLIC, Dr. ROBERT DURAND AND COLLABORATORS

Why are health professionals burning out while they give the best of themselves to heal the world? Dr. Bak aims to break the curse of isolation that health professionals face and establish a conversation to start the healing process. PROFESSION HEALTH is the basis of an ongoing discussion and will also serve as an introduction to a study lead by Professor Robert Durand, DMD, MSc Science from University of Montreal, study co-financed by Mdex and the Federal Government of Canada. Co-writers are Dr. Mirjana Sindolic, Professor Robert Durand, Dr. Jean De Serres, MD and former President of Hema Quebec, Counsel-Minister Luis Maria Kalaff Sanchez, Dr. Miguel Angel Russo, MD, Banker Anthony Siggia, Banker Kyles Yves, and more...
This is the first Tome of three, dedicated to help "WHITE COATS" to heal and to find their happiness.

# R

## REBOOT -012
### MIDLIFE CRISIS
BY Dr. BAK NGUYEN

MidLife Crisis is a common theme to each of us as we reach the threshold. As a man, as a woman, why is it that half of the marriages end up in recall? If anything else would have half those rates of failure, the lawsuits would be raining. Where are the flaws, the traps? Love is strong and pure, why is marriage not the reflection of that?

All hard to ask questions with little or no answers. Dr. Bak is sharing his reflections and findings as he reached himself the WALL OF MARRIAGE. This is a matter that affects all of our lives. It is time for some answers.

## RELEVANCY - TOME TWO -064
## REINVENTING OURSELVES TO SURVIVE
BY Dr. BAK NGUYEN & Dr. PAUL OUELLETTE AND COLLABORATORS

THE GREAT PAUSE was a reboot of all the systems of society. Many outdated systems will not make it back. The Dental Industry is a needed one, it has laid on complacency for far too long. In an age where expertise is global and democratized and can be replaced with technologies and artificial intelligence, the REBOOT will force, not just an update, but an operating system replacement and a firmware upgrade.First, they saved their industry with THE ALPHAS INITIATIVE, sharing their knowledge and vision freely to all the world's dental industry. With the OUELLETTE INITIATIVE, they bought some time to all the dental clinics to resume and to adjust. The warning has been given, the clock is now ticking. who will prevail and prosper and who will be left behind, outdated and obsolete?

## RISING -062
## TO WIN MORE THAN YOU ARE AFRAID TO LOSE
BY Dr. BAK NGUYEN

In RISING, TO WIN MORE TAN YOU ARE AFRAID TO LOSE, Dr. Bak is breaking down the strategy to success to all, not only those wearing white coats and scrubs.  More than his previous book (SUCCESS IS A CHOICE), this one is covering most of the aspects of getting to the next level, psychologically, socially, and financially.  Rising is broken down into three key strategies: Financial Leverage - Compressing time - Always being in control. Presented by MILLION DOLLAR MINDSET, the book is covering more than the ways to create wealth, but also how to reach happiness and to live a life without regrets. Dr. Bak the CEO and founder of Mdex & Co, a company with the promise of reforming the whole dental industry for the better. He wrote more than 60 books within 30 months as he is sharing his experiences, secrets, and wisdom.

# S

## SELFMADE -036
### GRATITUDE AND HUMILITY
BY Dr. BAK NGUYEN

This is the story of Dr. Bak, an artist who became a dentist, a dentist who became an Entrepreneur, an Entrepreneur who is seeking to save an entire industry.In his free time, Dr. Bak managed to write 37 books and is a contender to 3 world records to be confirmed. Businessman and visionary, his views and philosophy are ahead of our time. This is his 37th book. In SELFMADE, Dr. Bak is answering the questions most entrepreneurs want to know, the HOWTO and the secret recipes, not just to succeed, but to keep going no matter what! SELFMADE is the perfect read for any entrepreneurs, novices, and veterans.

## SUCCESS IS A CHOICE -060
### BLUEPRINTS FOR HEALTH PROFESSIONALS
BY Dr. BAK NGUYEN

In SUCCESS IS A CHOICE, FINANCIAL MILLIONAIRE BLUEPRINTS FOR HEALTH PROFESSIONALS, Dr. Bak is breaking down the strategy to success for all those wearing white coats and scrubs: doctors, dentists, pharmacists, chiropractors, nurses, etc. Success is broken down into three key strategies: Financial Leverage - Compressing time - Always being in control. Presented by MILLION DOLLAR MINDSET, the book is covering more than the ways to create wealth, but also how to reach happiness and to live a life without regrets.Dr. Bak is a successful cosmetic dentist with nearly 20 years of experience. He founded Mdex & Co, a company with the promise of reforming the whole dental industry for the better. While doing so, he discovered a passion for writing and for sharing. Multiple times World Record, Dr. Bak is writing a book every 2 weeks for the last 30 months. This is his 60th book, and he is still practicing. How he does it, is what he is sharing with us, SUCCESS, HAPPINESS, and mostly FREEDOM to all Health Professionals.

## SYMPHONY OF SKILLS -001
BY Dr. BAK NGUYEN

You will enlighten the world with your potential. I can't wait to see all the differences that you will have in our world. Remember that power comes with responsibility. We can feel in his presence, a genuine force, a depth of energy, confidence, innocence, courage, and intelligence. Bak is always looking for answers, morning and night, he wants to understand the why and the why not. This book is the essence of the man. Dr. Bak is a force of nature who bears proudly his title eHappy. The man never ceases smiling nor spreading his good vibe wherever he passes. He is not trapped in the nostalgia of the past nor the satisfaction of the present, he embodies the joy of what's possible, what's to come. The more we read, the more we share, and we live. That is Bak, he charms us to evolve and to share his points of view, and before we know it, we are walking by his side, a journey we never saw coming.

# T

## THE 90 DAYS CHALLENGE -061
BY Dr. BAK NGUYEN

THE 90 DAYS CHALLENGE, is Dr. Bak's journey into the unknown. Overachiever writing 2 books a month on average, for the last 30 months, ambitious CEO, Industries' Disruptor, Dr. Bak seems to have success in everything he touches. Everything except the control of his weight. For nearly 20 years, he struggles with an overweight problem. Every time he scored big, he added on a little more weight. Well, this time, he exposes himself out there, in real-time and without filter, accepting the challenge of his brother-in-law, DON VO to lose 45 pounds within 90 days. That's half a pound a day, for three months. He will have to do so while keeping all of his other challenges on track, writing books at a world record pace, leading the dental industry into the new ERA, and keep seeing his patients. Undoubtedly entertaining, this is the journey of an ALPHA who simply won't give up. But this time, nothing is sure.

## THE BOOK OF LEGENDS -024
BY Dr. BAK NGUYEN & WILLIAM BAK

The Book of Legends vol. 1 the story behind the world record of Dr. Bak and his son, William Bak. All Dr. Bak had in mind was to keep his promise of writing a book with his son. They ended up writing 8 children's books within a month, scoring a new world record. William is also the youngest author having published in two languages. Those are world records waiting to be confirmed. History will say: to celebrate a first world record (writing 15 books / 15 months), for the love of his son, he will have scored a second world record: to write 8 books within a month! THE BOOK OF LEGENDS vol. 1 This is both a magical journey for both a father and a son looking to connect and to find themselves. Join Dr. Bak and William Bak in their journey and their love for Life!

## THE BOOK OF LEGENDS 2 -041
BY Dr. BAK NGUYEN & WILLIAM BAK

THE BOOK OF LEGENDS vol. 2 is the sequel of "CINDERELLA" but a true story between a father and his son. Together they have discovered a bond and a way to connect. The first BOOK OF LEGENDS covered the time of the first four books they wrote together within a month. The second BOOK OF LEGENDS is covering what happened after the curtains dropped, what happened after reality kicked back in. If the first volume was about a fairy tale in vacation time, the second volume is about making it last in real Life. Share their journey and their love of Life!

## THE BOOK OF LEGENDS 3 -086
### THE END OF THE INNOCENCE AGE
BY Dr. BAK NGUYEN & WILLIAM BAK

This is the third volume of the series, THE BOOK OF LEGENDS. If the first two happened as a breeze breaking world records on top of world records (27 books written as father and son), the 3rd volume took much more time to arrive. William has grown and writing chicken books is not enough anymore to ignite his imagination. Dr. Bak, as a good father, will try to follow William's growth and invented new games, technics and mind frames to keep engaging William's imagination and interest. From auditions to backstories, Dr. Bak bent backward to keep the adventure going. More than sharing the success and the glory, within THE BOOK OF LEGENDS volume 3, you are sharing the doubts and failure of a father and son refusing to let go... but who have now left MOMENTUM... until the winds blow once more in their favour. Welcome to the Alphas.

## THE CONFESSION OF A LAZY OVERACHIEVER -089
### REINVENT YOURSELF FROM ANY CRISIS
BY Dr. BAK NGUYEN

In THE CONFESSION OF A LAZY OVERACHIEVER, Dr. Bak is opening up to his new marketing officer, Jamie, fresh out of school. She is young, full of energy, and looking to chill and still to have it all. True to his character, Dr. Bak is giving Jamie some leeway to redefine Dr. Bak's brand to her demographic, the Millennials. This journey is about Dr. Bak satisfying the Millennials and answering their true questions in life. A rebel himself, his ambition to change the world started back on campus, some 25 years ago... then, life caught up with him. It took Dr. Bak 20 years to shake down the burdens of life, to spread his wings free from Conformity, and to start Overachieving. Doctor, CEO, and world record author, here is what Dr. Bak would have love to know 25 years ago as was still on campus. In a word, this is cheating your way to success and freedom. And yes, it is possible. Success, Money, Freedom, it all starts with a mindset and the awareness of Time. Welcome to the Alphas.

## THE ENERGY FORMULA -053
BY Dr. BAK NGUYEN

THE ENERGY FORMULA is a book dedicated to help each individual to find the means to reach their purpose and goal in Life. Dr. Bak is a philosopher, a strategist, a business, an artist, and a dentist, how does he do all of that? He is doing so while mentoring proteges and leading the modernization of an entire industry. Until now, Momentum and Speed were the powers that he was building on and from. But those powers come from somewhere too. From a guide of our Quest of Identity, he became an ally in everyone's journey for happiness. THE ENERGY FORMULA is the book revealing step by step, the logic of building the right mindset and the way to ABUNDANCE and HAPPINESS, universally. It is not just a HOW TO book, but one that will change your life and guide you to the path of ABUNDANCE.

## THE MODERN WOMAN -070
### TO HAVE IT HAVE WITH NO SACRIFICE
BY Dr. BAK NGUYEN & Dr. EMILY LETRAN

In THE MODERN WOMAN: TO HAVE IT ALL WITH NO SACRIFICE, Dr. Bak joins forces with Dr. Emily Letran to empower all women to fulfill their desires, goals, and ambition. Both overachievers going against the odds, they are sharing their experience and wisdom to help all women to find confidence and support to redefine their lives. Dr. Emily Letran is a doctor in dentistry, an entrepreneur, author, and CERTIFIED HIGH-PERFORMANCE coach. For an Asian woman, she made it through the norms and the red tapes to find her voice. As she learned and grew with mentors, today she is sharing her secret with the energy that will motivate all of the female genders to stand for what they deserve. Alpha doctor, Bak is joining his voice and perspective since this is not about gender equality, but about personal empowerment and the quest of identity of each, man and woman. Once more, Dr. Bak is bringing LEVERAGE and REASON to the new social deal between man and woman. This is not about gender, but about confidence.

## THE POWER BEHIND THE ALPHA -008
BY TRANIE VO & Dr. BAK NGUYEN

It's been said by a "great man" that "We are born alone and we die alone." Both men and women proudly repeat those words as wisdom since. I apologize in advance, but what a fat LIE! That's what I learned and discovered in life since my mind and heart got liberated from the burden of scars and the ladders of society. I can have it all, not all at the same time, but I can have everything I put my mind and heart into. Actually, it is not completely true. I can have most of what I and Tranie put our minds into. Together, when we feel like one, there isn't much out of our reach. If I'm the mind, she's the heart; if I'm the Will, she's the means. Synergy is the core of our power. Tranie's aim is always Happiness. In Tranie's definition of life, there are no justifications, no excuses, no tomorrow. For Tranie, Happiness is measured by the minutes of every single day. This is why she's so strong and can heal people around her. That may also be why she doesn't need to talk much, since talking about the past or the future is, in her mind, dimming down the magic of the present, the Now. We both respect and appreciate that we are the whole balancing each other's equation of life, of love, of success. I was the plus and the minus, then I became the multiplication factor and grew into the exponential. And how is Tranie evolving in all of this? She is and always will be the balance. If anything, she is the equal sign of each equation.

## THE POWER OF Dr. -066
### THE MODERN TITLE OF NOBILITY
BY Dr. BAK NGUYEN, Dr. PAVEL KRASTEV AND COLLABORATORS

In THE POWER OF Dr., independent thinkers mean to exchange ideas. An idea can be very powerful if supported with a great work ethic. Work ethic, isn't that the main fabric of our white coats, scrubs, and title? In an era post-COVID where everything has been rebooted and that the healthcare industry is facing its own fate: to evolve or to be replaced, Dr. Bak and Dr. Pavel reveal the source of their power and their playbook to move forward, ahead. The power we all hold is our resilience and discipline. We put that for years at the service of our profession, from a surgical perspective. Now, we can harness that same power to rewrite the rules, the industry, and our future. Post-COVID, the rules are being rewritten, will you be part of the team or left behind?
"You can be in control!" More than personal growth and a motivational book, THE POWER OF Dr. is an awakening call to the doctor you look at when you graduate, with hope, with honour, with determination.

## THE POWER OF YES -010
### VOLUME ONE: IMPACT
BY Dr. BAK NGUYEN

In THE POWER OF YES, Dr. Bak is sharing his journey opening up and embracing the world, one day at a time, one ask at a time, one wish at a time. Far from a dare, saying YES allowed Dr. Bak to rewrite his mindsets and to break all the boundaries. This book is not one written a few days or weeks, but the accumulation of a journey for 12 months. The journeys started as Dr. Bak said YES to his producer to go on stage and to speak... That YES opened a world of possibilities. Dr. Bak embraced each and every one of them. 12 months later, he is celebrating the new world record of writing 9 books written over a period of 12 months. To him, it will be a miss, missing the 12 on 12 mark. To the rest of the world, they just saw the birth of a force of nature, the Alpha force. THE POWER OF YES is comprised of all the introduction of the adult books written by Dr. Bak within the first 12 months. Chapter by chapter, you can walk in his footstep seeing and smelling what he has. This is reality literature with a twist of POWER. THE POWER OF YES! Discover your potential and your power. This is the POWER OF YES, volume one. Welcome to the Alphas.

## THE POWER OF YES 2 -037
### VOLUME TWO: SHAPELESS
BY Dr. BAK NGUYEN

In THE POWER OF YES, volume 2, Dr. Bak is continuing his journey discovering his powers and influence. After 12 months embracing the world saying YES, he rose as an emerging force: he's been recognized as an INDUSTRIES DISRUPTOR, got nominated ERNST AND YOUNG ENTREPRENEUR OF THE YEAR, wrote 9 books within 12 months while launching the most ambitious private endeavour to reform his own industry, the dental field. Contender too many WORLD RECORDS, Dr. Bak is doing all of that in parallel. And yes, he is sleeping his nights and yes, he is writing his book himself, from the screen of his iPhone! Far from satisfied, Dr. Bak missed the mark of writing 12 books within 12 months and everything else is shaping and moving, and could come crumbling down at each turn. Now that Dr. Bak understands his powers, he is looking to test them and to push them to their limits, looking to keep scoring world records while materializing his vision and enterprises. This is the awakening of a Force of Nature looking to change the world for the better while having fun sharing. Welcome to the Alphas.

## THE POWER OF YES 3 -046
### VOLUME THREE: LIMITLESS
BY Dr. BAK NGUYEN

In THE POWER OF YES, volume 3, the journey of Dr. Bak continues where the last volume left, in front of 300 plus people showing up to his first solo event, a Dr. Bak's event. On stage and in this book, Dr. Bak reveals how 12 months saying YES to everything changed his life… actually, it was 18 months.
From a dentist looking to change the world from a dental chair into a multiple times world record author, the journey of openness is a rendez-vous with Fate. Dr. Bak is sharing almost in real-time his journey, experiences, but above all, his feelings, doubts, and comebacks. From one book to the next, from one journey to the next, follow the adventure of a man looking to find his name, his worth, and his place in the world. Doing so, he is touching people Doing so, he is touching people and initiating their rises. Are you ready for more? Are you ready to meet your Fate and Destiny? Welcome to the Alphas.

## THE POWER OF YES 4 -087
### VOLUME FOUR: PURPOSE
BY Dr. BAK NGUYEN

In THE POWER OF YES, volume 4, the journey continues days after where the last volume left. After setting the new world record of writing 48 books within 24 months, Dr. Bak is not ready to stop. As volume one covers 12 months of journey, volume 2 covers 6 months. Well, volume 3 covers 4 months. The speed is building up and increasing, steadily. This is volume 4, RISING, after breaking the sound barrier. Dr. Bak has reached a state where he is above most resistance and friction, he is now in a universe of his own, discovering his powers as he walks his journeys. This is no fiction story or wishful thinking, THE POWER OF YES is the journey of Dr. Bak, from one world record to the next, from one book to the next. You too can walk your own legend, you just need to listen to your innersole and to open up to the opportunity. May you get inspiration from the legendary journey of Dr. Bak and find your own Destiny. Welcome to the Alphas.

## THE RISE OF THE UNICORN -038
BY Dr. BAK NGUYEN & Dr. JEAN DE SERRES

In THE RISE OF THE UNICORN, Dr. Bak is joining forces with his friend and mentor, Dr. Jean De Serres. Together both men had many achievements in their respective industries, but the advent of eHappyPedia, THE RISE OF THE UNICORN is a personal project dear to both of them: the QUEST OF HAPPINESS and its empowerment. This book is a special one since you are witnessing the conversation between two entrepreneurs looking to change the world by building unique tools and media. Just like any enterprise, the ride is never a smooth one in the park on a beautiful day. But this is about eHappyPedia, it is about happiness, right? So it will happen and with a smile attached to it! The unique value of this book is that you are sharing the ups and downs of the launch of a Unicorn, not just the glory of the fame, but also the doubts and challenges on the way. May it inspire you on your own journey to success and happiness.

## THE RISE OF THE UNICORN 2 -076
## eHappyPedia
BY Dr. BAK NGUYEN & Dr. JEAN DE SERRES

This is 2 years after starting the first tome. Dr. Bak's brand is picking up, between the accumulation of records and the recognition. eHappyPedia is now hot for a comeback. In THE RISE OF THE UNICORN 2, Dr. Bak is retracing and addressing each of Dr. Jean De Serres' concerns about the weakness of the first version of eHappyPedia and the eHappy movement. This is the sort of the creation and a UNICORN both in finance and in psychology. Never before, you will assist in such daily and decision-making process of a world phenomenon and of a company. Dr. Bak and Dr. De Serres are literally using the process of writing this series of books to plan and to brainstorm the birth of a bluechip. More than an intriguing story, this is the journey of 2 experienced entrepreneurs changing the world.

## THE U.A.X STORY -072
## THE ULTIMATE AUDIO EXPERIENCE
BY Dr. BAK NGUYEN

This is the story of the ULTIMATE AUDIO EXPERIENCE, U.A.X. Follow Dr. Bak's footstep on how he invented a new way to read and to learn. Dr. Bak brings his experience as a movie producer and a director to elevate the reading experience to another level with entertaining value and make it accessible to everyone, auditive, and visual people alike.

Three years plus of research and development, countless hours of trials and errors, Dr. Bak finally solved his puzzle: having written more than 1.1 million words. The irony is that he does not like to read, he likes audiobooks! U.A.X. finally allowed the opening of Dr. Bak's entire library to a new genre and media. U.A.X. is the new way to learn and enjoy Audiobooks. Made to be entertaining while keeping the self-educational value of a book, U.A.X. will appeal to both auditive and visual people. U.A.X. is the blockbuster of the Audiobooks. The format has already been approved by iTunes, Amazon, Spotify, and all major platforms for global distribution and streaming.

## THE VACCINE -077
BY Dr. BAK NGUYEN & WILLIAM BAK

In THE VACCINE, A TALE OF SPIES AND ALIENS, Dr. Bak reprise his role as mentor to William, his 10 years-old son, both as co-author and as doctor. William is living through the COVID war and has accumulated many, many questions. That morning, they got out all at once. From a conversation between father and son, Dr. Bak is making science into words keeping the interest of his son a Saturday morning in bed. William is not just an audience, he is responsible to map the field with his questions. What started as a morning conversation between father and son, became within the next hour, a great project, their 23rd book together. Learn about the virus, vaccination while entertaining your kids.

## TO OVERACHIEVE EVERYTHING BEING LAZY -090
## CHEAT YOUR WAY TO SUCCESS
BY Dr. BAK NGUYEN

In TO OVERACHIEVE EVERYTHING BEING LAZY, Dr. Bak retaking his role talking to the millennials, the next generation. If in the first tome of the series LAZY, Dr. Bak addresses the general audience of millennials, especially young women, he is dedicating this tome to the ALPHA amongst the millennials, those aiming for the moon and looking, not only to be happy but to change the world. This is not another take on how to cheat your way to success or how to leverage laziness, but this is the recipe to build overachievers and rainmakers. For the young leaders with ambitions and talent, understanding TIME and ENERGY are crucial from your first steps writing your our legend. If Dr. Bak had the chance to do it all over again, this is how he would do it! Welcome to the Alphas.

## TORNADO -067
## FORCE OF CHANGE
BY Dr. BAK NGUYEN

In TORNADO - FORCE OF CHANGE Dr. Bak is writing solo. In the midst of the COVID war, change is not a good intention anymore. Change, constant change has become a new reality, a new norm. From somebody who holds the title of Industries' Disruptor, how does he yield change to stay in control? Well, the changes from the COVID war are constant fear and much loss of individual liberty. Some can endure the change, some will ride it. Dr. Bak is sharing his angle of navigating the changes, yielding the improvisations, and to reinvent the goals, the means to stay relevant. From fighting to keep his companies Dr. Bak went on to let go the uncontrollable to embrace the opportunity, he reinvented himself to ride the change and create opportunities from an unprecedented crisis. This is the story of a man refusing to kneel and accept defeat, smiling back at faith to find leverage and hope.

## TOUCHSTONE -073
## LEVERAGING TODAY'S PSYCHOLOGICAL SMOG
BY Dr. BAK NGUYEN & Dr. KEN SEROTA

TOUCHSTONE, LEVERAGING TODAY'S PSYCHOLOGICAL SMOG is mapping to navigate and to thrive in today's high and constant stress environment. After 40 years in practice, Dr. Serota is concerned about the evolution of the career of health care professionals and the never-ending level of stress. What is stress, what are its effects, damages, and symptoms? If COVID-19 revealed to the world that we are fragile, it also revealed most of the broken and the flaws of our system. For now a century, dentistry has been a champion in depression, Dr.ug addiction, and suicide rate, and the curve is far from flattening. Dr. Bak is sharing his perspective and experience dealing with stress and how to leverage it into a constructive force. From the stress of a doctor with no right to failure to the stress of an entrepreneur never knowing the future, Dr. Bak is sharing his way to use stress as leverage.

From Canada, **Dr BAK NGUYEN**, Nominee Ernst and Young Entrepreneur of the year, Grand Homage Lys DIVERSITY, and LinkedIn & TownHall Achiever of the year. Dr Bak is a cosmetic dentist, CEO and founder of Mdex & Co. His company is revolutionizing the dental field. Speaker and motivator, he wrote 72 books over 36 months accumulating many world records (to be officialized).

- **ENTREPRENEURSHIP**
- **LEADERSHIP**
- **QUEST OF IDENTITY**
- **DENTISTRY AND MEDICINE**
- **PARENTING**
- **CHILDREN BOOKS**
- **PHILOSOPHY**

In 2003, he founded Mdex, a dental company upon which in 2018, he launched the most ambitious private endeavour to reform the dental industry, Canada wide. Philosopher, he has close to his heart the quest of happiness of the people surrounding him, patients and colleagues alike. In 2020, he launched an International collaborative initiative named **THE ALPHAS** to share knowledge and for Entrepreneurs and Doctors to thrive through the Greatest Pandemic and Economic depression of our time.

In 2016, he co-found with Tranie Vo, Emotive World Incorporated, a tech research company to use technology to empower happiness and sharing. U.A.X. the ultimate audio experience is the landmark project on which the team is advancing, utilizing the technics of the movie industry and the advancement in ARTIFICIAL INTELLIGENCE to save the book industry and to upgrade the continuing education space.

These projects have allowed Dr Nguyen to attract interests from the international and diplomatic community and he is now the center of a global discussion in the wellbeing and the future of the health profession. It is in that matter that he shares his thoughts and encourages the health community to share their own stories.

"It's not worth it go through it alone! Together, we stand, alone, we fall."

Motivational speaker and serial entrepreneur, philosopher and author, from his own words, Dr Nguyen describes himself as a dentist by circumstances, an entrepreneur by nature and a communicator by passion.

He also holds recognitions from the Canadian Parliament and the Canadian Senate.

www.DrBakNguyen.com

# UAX

## ULTIMATE AUDIO EXPERIENCE

A new way to learn and enjoy Audiobooks. Made to be entertaining while keeping the self-educational value of a book, UAX will appeal to both auditive and visual people. UAX is the blockbuster of the Audiobooks.

UAX will cover most of Dr Bak's books, and is now negotiating to bring more authors and more titles to the UAX concept. Now streaming on Spotify, Apple Music and available for download on all major music platforms. Give it a try today!

AMAZON - BARNES & NOBLE - APPLE BOOKS - KINDLE
SPOTIFY - APPLE MUSIC

www.DrBakNguyen.com

# CHILDREN'S BOOK
with William Bak

## The Trilogy of Legends

## THE SPIES AND ALIENS COLLECTION

SHORTCUT                     SOCIETY

DR.

*Bak Nguyen*